In Harmony with your Horse

IN HARMONY WITH YOUR HORSE

HOW TO BUILD A LASTING RELATIONSHIP

BY CLARE ALBINSON

THE LYONS PRESS
GUILFORD, CONNECTICUT
An imprint of The Globe Pequot Press

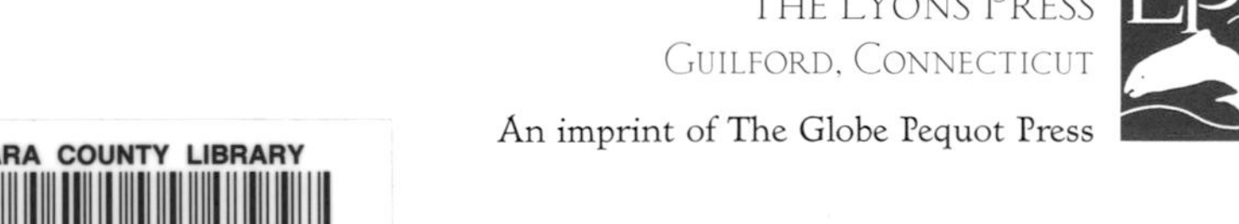

Design by LeAnna Weller Smith

The Lyons Press is an imprint of The Globe Pequot Press.

10 9 8 7 6 5 4 3 2 1

ISBN 1-58574-675-4

Printed in the United States of America

Library of Congress Cataloging-in-Publication data is available on file.

Contents

Why did I write this Book?

"… horses should be trained in such a way that they not only love their riders, but look forward to the time they are with them."

Xenophon, 400 B.C.

"We must strive for a greater understanding of the nature of our horse, his method of communication and the mechanics of his body. Most importantly we need to recognize the effect we can have on all of these. With this knowledge we can more happily coexist and more successfully work together."

Author

We have all had the lessons, read the books and gone to the lectures. We try so hard to understand what they mean and we try to do as they say but still we don't produce horses like the top trainers. Why? What is the magic ingredient? Surely not lack of dedication, because riders are usually a very committed group of people. We tend to be well informed and so many of us watch videos and read books on the subject and have many lessons; yet success still eludes us. Why should

this be? I came to the conclusion that, despite having the information at our disposal, there isn't a total understanding of that information. Perhaps fuller, better, easier to understand explanations would help us struggling equestrians learn faster.

My starting point on this book came several years ago when I volunteered to give talks on dressage to the members of our local Pony Club. I wanted to create lighthearted and illuminating descriptions for the talks. Explanations occurred to me which, I felt, made what was being described surprisingly clear. At the end of

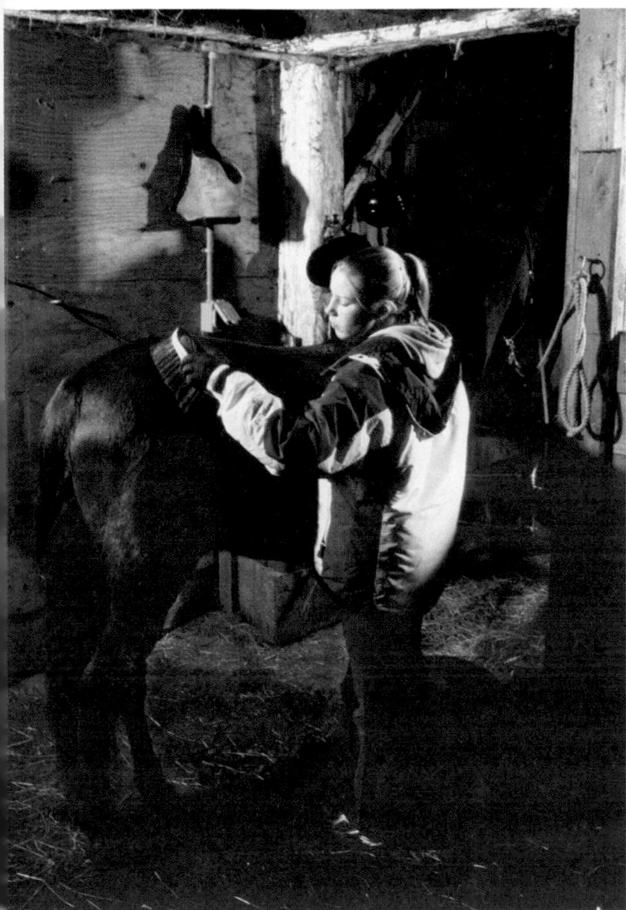

the process I was amazed to find that I too had come to a better understanding of that which I was describing. At this time I was concentrating on information that explores a better understanding of the balance of the rider and the balance of the horse, how they can both be improved through training and also how the rider's balance can affect that of the horse. Understanding these concepts is fundamental to the training of the horse.

I came to realize, though, that we also need to know more about the mentality of our horses. We need to know how they relate to and communicate with each other, and therefore with us. We need to develop sympathetic training techniques that benefit both ourselves and our horses. With a better understanding of the horse's mind and an improved ability to communicate, misunderstandings between us should be reduced and our relationship improved. Schooling should become a pleasant, productive time. Understanding the instinctive behavior of horses, and the ability to use this knowledge when schooling them, can bring enormous benefits both to the speed of progress with your work as well as to the level of enjoyment you experience.

Reading this book should, hopefully, lead you to a deeper understanding of the basic balance of both you and your horse. Because you understand more about this, you will be able to direct your energy to where it is needed. The book should also lead you to better understand the mind and behavior of your horse. If you know more about his personality, you should discover a kinder, more intelligent approach to horse training and handling and gain a new insight into how to get the best out of your relationship.

CHAPTER 1

The Nature of Horses

If you understand the nature and behavior of horses you will get the best out of them, both as friends and as athletes. If you know what they do in certain circumstances, and why they do it, training them is much easier and more successful. Because you understand them better, you will develop a closer relationship and you will both enjoy each other's company more!

Much of the horse's behavior is innate. It is inborn, instinctive behavior, derived from their existence when living in the wild. They developed this over thousands of years in order to survive in a harsh, cruel environment. Though they have been domesticated for a long time, this instinctive behavior has not left them. We must strive to understand it, because it forms as much a part of them as their desire to eat and to sleep. We need to research and examine it closely, because it forms the pegs upon which we will hang the development of their training. It is not possible to go against the nature of the horse. We have to accept, understand and work with them as they are.

To train horses as efficiently and effectively as possible, we must understand how they learn, and, based on this, use the best methods to teach them.

Humans are often guilty of anthropomorphism: we like to give our animals the characters of humans. We must take care not to fall into the trap of always believing they think and behave as we do. We must maintain an awareness of their true nature. However, there are certain ways in which humans and horses are similar; for example, in their need for companionship, their social order and their body language. It is largely because of these similarities that humans and horses get on so well with each other.

PEACEFUL, SOCIABLE SURVIVAL

Horses are by nature gentle creatures: they eat grass and they do not kill other animals. They do not normally need aggression to survive. If threatened they will flee—and because they are so fast, they will outrun most of their predators.

The main aim in the lives of horses is to survive both as individuals and as a breed. To survive as a breed they need to mate and reproduce. To survive as an individual they need to be able to find food and recognize their predators: to see or hear them coming and to run away. This is why they are social animals. It is essential to their survival. All members of the herd are on the lookout for threatening situations. Because there are many horses in the herd, each looking in a different direction while they graze, they have a better chance of seeing, hearing or smelling a potential threat than a lone animal would have. Being in a group also deters a potential predator who might consider taking on a vulnerable lone animal, but not a group. A lone horse would not survive for long in the wild and he knows it. A predator may attack and kill him if he lacks the protection of the herd. If he was part of a group, a predator would know that the combined forces of the herd would easily fight him off, and possibly injure him. So he keeps away.

So a horse has a strong instinct to belong to a group. To be isolated could mean death. Because of this, all horses crave company. It is this instinct—to have company and be part of a group—that holds the group together and forms the basis of their social structure. Horses within a group frequently reinforce this social structure by mutual grooming. They first touch noses and, provided there has been no

objection from either of them, they will go on to groom each other on their manes, withers and sometimes croup. They are effectively saying that they are friends, and that they will look out for each other. This process initiates or reinforces their relationship, which makes them care about each other and want to stick together as a group. It is often described as bonding. They are rather like the members of a large family, all loving each other and looking out for each other (though not necessarily

liking each other!). They will also pair off and form lasting friendships with particular horses. This will often be with horses of a similar age and maybe the same sex. They are not unlike humans in this way. During the ritual of mutual grooming, the heartbeat of both horses will drop as they become more relaxed. Horses will eventually mutually groom with all the members of their group, thus reinforcing the bond between the whole group. They will mutually groom with the rest of the group much less often than with their specific friends. These friendships are very important to horses, and they will display a strong desire to be reunited with their "friend," if they are separated, by calling loudly and by showing agitation.

When horses initiate or reestablish their relationship they often touch noses. The horse's mouth and nose are very responsive to touch and smell. They are the most sensitive parts of the animal, with many, many nerve endings capable of sending to their brain detailed messages about the surface and smell of what they are investigating. This helps them perform delicate tasks with their mouth, such as selecting the best grass from among the weeds.

The nose and mouth are the first parts of another horse's anatomy that a horse will allow into his personal space, before checking him out and letting him further in. The horse uses his outstretched nose and mouth to sense what the other animal is—keeping him at his distance until he is sure. This gesture roughly compares to the human handshake; they are touching, and giving out messages of civility and friendship, but in fact still sizing each other up. The nose and mouth are also areas used by horses to give reassurance (and perhaps affection) to another horse, as with a mare touching her foal. The next stage would be when the horse lets the other horse further into his space, and they mutually groom each other. Now they are two best mates with their arms round one another.

Because it is such an important part of horses' survival, they are programmed to have a strong need for familiar equine company. If deprived of the company of other horses, they will soon make similar lasting friendships with other animals, including humans. Their strong need for company eventually overcomes the desire for the specific company of a horse, and they will make do with just about anyone. Their instinct tells them that to survive they must have company, even if it is not equine.

RECOGNITION

The ability to recognize others is essential if this social system is to work. There is no doubt that horses show a marked ability to recognize other horses by using their visual, auditory and olfactory (smell) senses, all of which are well developed.

DOMINATION

Within the group, horses will develop a pecking order. A hierarchy evolves. Each horse knows where he stands in relation to all the other horses in the group in different circumstances. This dominance is based on the threat of violence from the dominant horse, and on the subservient animal's fear of it. (In the lower orders of human life this still occurs, but in more civilized society the violence or threat of violence has been replaced by outward manifestations of superiority, such as a cultured voice or an expensive car.) Once the domination is established between horses, it is actually a way of avoiding violence. Each animal knows his place in the hierarchy and will respect the dominance of other animals in order to avoid being hurt. Simply placing his ears back will often be enough for a dominant horse to remind another of his subservience. Occasionally the domination of one animal by another may be challenged, particularly as the younger horses mature and the older ones become weaker. Presumably the normally subservient horse always has his eyes open for a chink in the armor of the dominating horse, though, as with humans, some horses are happier in the lower part of the pecking order. Life is often easier there!

At times this hierarchy can be upset by bonding. A horse from lower down in the rankings may bond with a horse who is dominant. While those two horses are together, the lower-ranking horse will take on the protection of the higher-ranking one and gain respect from those who would normally dominate him. Because of this, it pays a horse to bond with those who are dominant. He gains from the strength and protection of this higher-ranking companion. Horses, rather like humans, will choose a powerful dominant friend if they have the chance. This is why it pays humans to be strong, powerful and dominant with their horses. Their strength makes the prospect of bonding with them more attractive to the horse.

VIOLENCE AND THE HORSE

Discipline and social order are an essential feature in the life of horses, but the horse rarely wishes to be violent for the sake of violence. He uses the threat of it to maintain his domination and gain the benefits of his superiority, such as to be the first to get to the hay or whatever. If, however, his threat is ignored, he will resort to violence to maintain his position or to control the situation. For example a horse will often kick out at another horse, even his own "friends" or offspring, if they overstep the mark or invade his space without permission. In the same way a mare will sometimes bite her own foal if he misbehaves or annoys her.

MATRIARCHAL MARE

Because horses are such social animals, they need a social code within the group so that they can peacefully coexist. The hierarchical system combined with the social system achieves this for most of the time, but beyond this there is a need for group leaders, or a "policeman" of the social code. This is often a matriarchal mare. She is the schoolmistress of the outfit, responsible for organizing the horses in

the group. She sometimes uses aggression to dominate its unruly members. As spotted by Monty Roberts, the original "horse whisperer," in extreme cases she uses isolation as a punishment and pushes out a troublemaker, keeping him away from the group and isolating him from their protection. He, knowing this to be a threat of death, will eventually signal to her that he will behave and she will let him back into the herd.

STALLION

The stallion's main function is to get the mares of his group pregnant. He also uses his superior strength, where necessary, to fight off both equine rivals and nonequine aggressors. He is responsible for maintaining the quality of the offspring of the group by making sure he (the best) is the father of them. Nature puts upon him the responsibility of keeping away and, if necessary, fighting off other stallions, to stop the possibility of his mares producing offspring from an inferior mate.

FLIGHT ANIMALS

Horses are flight animals: their first reaction is to run away from things that frighten them. If they hear or see something they are unfamiliar with, instead of investigating it, they run away and ask questions later. If they feel pain, they almost always instinctively run—rather than fighting the source of the pain.

MEMORY

Horses have exceptional memories—like elephants, they never forget. In the wild they use their memories to relocate to watering holes and good grazing. They also need to remember, and recognize, their mates and companions. They never seem to forget a lesson, once it is learned, nor a face, a place or a bad experience.

COMMUNICATION

Horses have limited vocal language, extending only to the whinny, the nicker, the hard blow and the squeal. Because they are such social animals they need to communicate with each other to a greater degree than this limited vocal language will allow. So, they have evolved a means of communication with their bodies and their faces. Sometimes this body language is very readable, such as when a horse bares his teeth, or turns his quarters in the direction of his victim. Sometimes it is very subtle, as when a horse lowers his head to avoid confrontation. Because this subject is so important and so complex I have devoted a separate chapter to it (chapter 4).

SMELL

Horses have a sense of smell that is vastly better than our own. They can tell who passed by quite a long time ago. If the wind is in the right direction, they may be able to tell where that animal is, even at quite a distance away. If a (forgive the pun) passing horse leaves droppings on the ground, another horse of his acquaintance could identify him from these droppings, even if they have been overlaid by other droppings. Horses recognize the smell of other horses and other animals on our clothes, or even the smell of familiar places.

FREQUENT EXPOSURE

When horses are repeatedly subjected to something which they would normally find frightening, but which doesn't harm them, they learn to ignore it. For example, if they heard a loud noise in the field beside them, horses grazing would undoubtedly run away from it. If this noise happened again, they would probably still run away. Suppose the noise was repeated day after day, and the horses had not been harmed in any way. After about a week the horses would cease to run away, and possibly even to acknowledge it. They have learned that, because the noise didn't cause them any harm, it was not worth wasting energy running away from it. A typical example is where a horse is put into a field with a railway line beside it. At first the horse is startled by the sight and sound of a train. After a few days he will not even lift his head when a train passes by. It is important that the noise (or whatever) is repeated many times during a short period. If it had happened as many times but over a longer period they would not become as accustomed to it. For example, if a loud noise had been repeated once a month, for six or seven months, the horses would probably still run away from it each time they heard it.

HOW DO HORSES LEARN?

Horses are very clever at associating related events. They learn what to expect in certain situations, and, therefore, how to react. Imagine that a horse heard a dog growling, followed by the appearance of a dog who then rushed out and bit him. The horse will remember that every time he hears a dog growling, he should move out of the way first—just in case the dog bites him.

A dominant member of the herd might flatten his ears when another horse came too near. If the less dominant herd member hadn't been aware of the meaning of this signal, and didn't move out of the way, he would probably end up being kicked. He would learn by association that when a horse puts his ears back, it means keep out of the way. In other words, the horse learns that when one thing happens, it is often followed by another related occurrence. If the horse learns that things that no longer used to be a danger now are, he may save his life by learning to run away from the new threat. Similarly, if he learns that a thing that used to be a threat no longer is, he will save valuable energy by not running away from it any more.

In their search for good food or water, horses will remember their location by associating features of the landscape with the food or water. One of the purposes of learning is survival. A horse's ability to learn from experience has helped him to survive as a breed, and we can use it in our efforts to train him.

VISION

A horse's vision is different from ours: he can see almost 360 degrees around him. He is blind only in about 3 degrees immediately behind his head. Because his eyes are situated on

the sides of his head he is also unable to see in a tiny wedge right in front of his nose. The right eye will see virtually all that is immediately in front of him, including approximately 32 degrees to the left of his nose. He will also see to the side, and behind him, but will see this with only one eye. The left eye will see the same on the left side. Apart from the small blind spot in front of his nose, the 65 degrees in front of the horse is seen with both eyes (binocular vision) and hence virtually everything within this area is seen clearly. Apart from the blind spot behind the horse all else is seen with only one eye, either the right or the left, which is obviously not as good as vision with two eyes. Using this monocular method, the horse has peripheral sight that allows him to see almost immediately behind him. But the further to the back of him that he looks, the more the image becomes blurred. Something that is behind him looks distorted. It is therefore more likely to give a horse a fright than something closer to the front. If the horse is unable to identify it, he will presume it is dangerous and shy away to a position where he can see it better.

A horse's vision is not as good as ours in daylight, but, due to the construction of his eye, he is better able to make use of the limited light available at night. Hence his night vision is better than ours.

HEARING

There is nothing to suggest that horses' hearing is particularly well developed, or greatly superior to our own, but horses definitely rely on their hearing to know what is going on around them, particularly if there is any threat of approaching danger. Their ears are especially flexible. Because of this, and the shape of the ear, their hearing is very directional. The ears can turn to the direction of the sound to hear it even better.

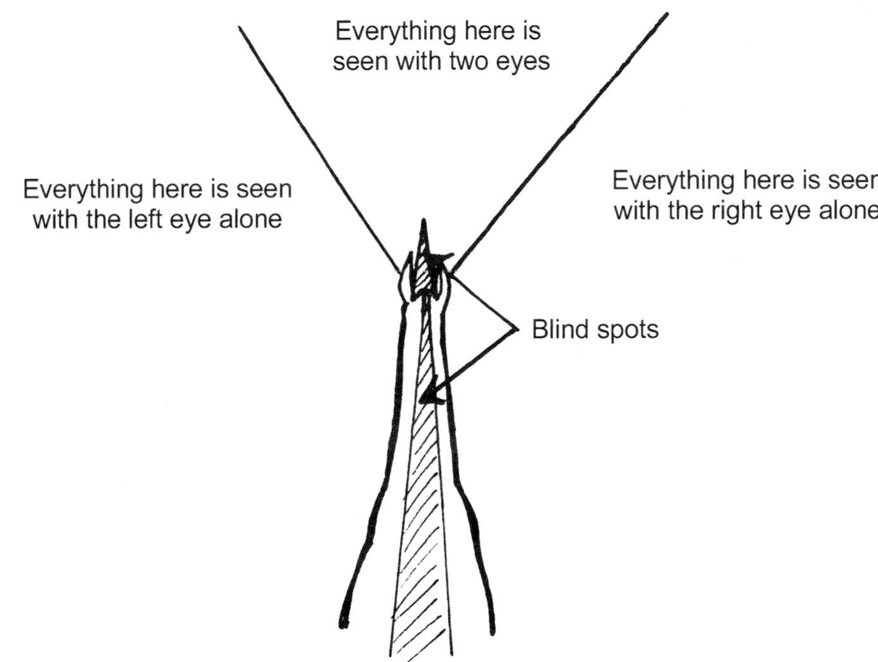

Fig. 1 The vision of the horse.

CHAPTER 2

Working with the Horse's Nature

The knowledge we have acquired about horses now needs to be applied to our relationship with them.

KEEPING CLOSE TO NATURE

In his natural environment the horse moves around with a group of other horses. He spends his entire day eating, resting and sleeping in the outdoors. In this outdoor life he wanders freely and constantly has the companionship of other horses.

We use horses for our benefit, not for theirs, so to suit our needs we change their environment. Instead of being out at grass all day, some horses spend part or all of their lives in a stable, eating dried grass and concentrated food. The better quality food makes them able to perform better, and the reduced eating time makes them more available for work. To a greater or lesser degree it is inevitable that we make our horses live in an unnatural environment. But, the more we interfere with their natural lifestyle, the more risk we run of psychological damage manifesting itself in bad habits, vices, tension, etc. If we can keep their living conditions as close to nature as possible, the horse should have a more balanced personality.

Some owners hardly let the horse out of the stable except to work. This is to reserve his energy and enthusiasm for work, and to stop him from hurting himself when running around in the field. If these horses were allowed to run round in a field every day for at least an hour or two, they arguably might end up being happier, working harder and performing better. Nevertheless there are some horses who take to permanent life in a stable like a duck to water, strongly resisting the potential hazards of the elements when offered them—particularly if it is raining!

It isn't always possible, but if we can also provide our horses with company in their field, preferably equine, they will be much happier. It is the natural lifestyle of the species, and the one in which they will be most relaxed. Again, some horses prove the exception to the rule and

prefer life on their own, particularly if they have the constant attention of an adoring owner.

One cruel tradition that exists is to wean foals from their mothers by locking them in a stable for days on end without any company whatsoever. The foals are terrified and desperately lonely. It is so unnecessary. If the foal has other company in the field that he is used to, and happy with, he will settle very well with this company if his

mother is taken away. It can be made even less of a shock to the foal if his mother has previously been taken away from him for short periods, so that he has had a chance to experience life without her before the extended separation at weaning.

USING THE HORSE'S SOCIAL CODE

There is something very special about the way in which horses relate to each other. Their system of discipline and social order makes it easy for us to dominate them in order to train them. Their ability to learn from associations and repeated exposure makes them good pupils. Their social code is tailor-made for us to step in and become part of it.

The importance of this social conditioning is borne out by the subsequent behavior of foals who are hand reared by humans. They frequently grow up very difficult to handle. It is as if they think of themselves as human, not horse, and expect to play life by our rules. They haven't learned the socializing skills of horses, which are fundamental to our ability to school them. In view of this, one might wonder just how important it is for us to handle young horses, particularly foals? Is it possible we may be interfering in the socializing process that is taught by other horses at this time? Should we leave nature to take its course and reap the benefits later, or do young horses benefit from being handled by humans frequently? I suspect that it is more beneficial to handle young stock, provided it is handled with proper respect for the discipline and social order of the species. If, in your handling of a young horse, you do not reinforce the discipline of the herd, you may well be teaching it a bad lesson for life. If you let a foal think that a human is normally dominated by the horse, it may be difficult to reverse this belief later.

The main aim in horses' lives has not changed with domesticity. They still have a strong drive to survive both as a species and individually—just like all animals. Obviously their sexual drive has survived intact, which is why we geld young male horses who are not needed for breeding. We fear that their attention may be diverted to sexual matters when they should be working for us.

Their instincts tell them that to survive as an individual they have to find food, water and companionship. Their life, domesticated by humans, normally gives them all of these.

SOCIAL ORGANIZATION

The desire of horses to have company, and bond with their companions, still exists in domestication. Because we are their close companions, they can and will bond with us just as they bond with their equine companions. Part of the bonding process that horses go through is their grooming of each other around the neck and wither. When you groom your horse you are not only cleaning him; you are nurturing the relationship between the two of you. Horses groom each other in the specified area which they "allow" the other horse into. When we groom, we go beyond the frontiers of this area, grooming all over the body. Often horses resent this. By making them accept it, we are both establishing and/or reestablishing our mutual trust and also our domination of them. This also applies when we stroke our horses.

If we are brave enough to confront horses and dominate them, this makes us a more desirable friend. They know that we will also be strong enough and brave enough to protect them. While we maintain this domination and strength, their desire to keep us a friend will remain. Add this to the closeness that is achieved by bonding with our horses, and we have the perfect combination to have a happy, compliant horse.

The nose and the mouth of the horse have something in common with the hands of humans. If we are meeting a new horse, or saying hello to our horse in the morning, placing our hand on his nose is seen by him as a greeting. We want him to let us happily into his personal space and accept us as his friend. We are merely aping nature and making him feel as comfortable as possible in our company. The next stage in the greeting is to groom our horse, particularly around the withers and neck. We know his heartbeat will become lower and he should become even more relaxed in our company. Just as horses strengthen their relationship by grooming each other, we can also strengthen our relationship with horses by grooming and stroking them.

DOMINATION, THE HIERARCHICAL SYSTEM AND SEEKING A STRONG FRIEND THROUGH BONDING

Horses would rather bond with another horse who is well up in the pecking order: a strong, dominant horse. He will share the dominant horse's social status when he is with him, and he will have his protection if threatened. Through bonding with horses we can achieve the closeness to them that they would normally reserve for other horses. This may occur even more so because we supply their food, but also because of the role we take on, the role of a dominant trainer. If we can replace the dominant horse by being a dominant, strong trainer, our horse will be happy to have our company. We can become his special friend, whom he will want to obey because he wants to retain our protective friendship.

A horse will seek our company because of the strength we manifest in dominating him. Like a child he will feel safer with us. The stronger we are with him—the more decisions we make for him—the more relaxed he will be. He feels we will look after him.

Nonetheless, a horse will often test your strength if he sees you manifesting some weakness. He may put in a challenge to your supremacy. There are two reasons for this. Perhaps the horse is naturally dominant and wishes to be your boss. If this is the case, you may well have something of a fight on your hands as he may resort to violence to establish his dominance. Whatever he does, you must be prepared to prove to him that he is wrong and that you are the braver. Horses are great users of bluff to gain a better social

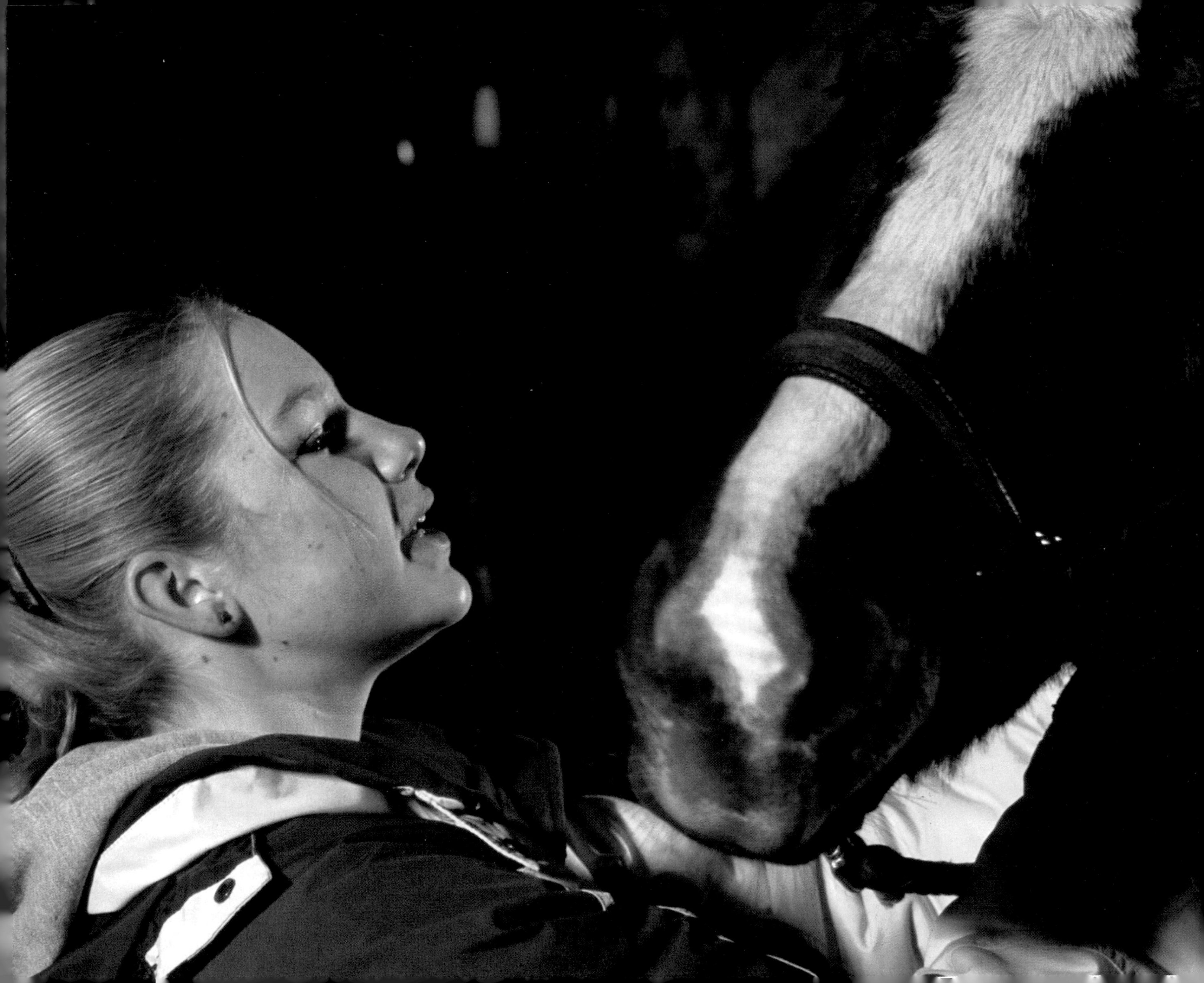

position. Humans can employ a similar subterfuge. Try to convince him that you are the dominant one by the body language you use. Occasionally, sadly, it may be necessary to use some physical punishment as proof if your bluff is called.

It could be that your behavior is the reason for the challenge. If you show weakness your horse may try to achieve supremacy. Perhaps you have flinched if he has turned his quarters towards you, and he has sensed your nervousness. He may wish himself to be on that higher plane, or he may be testing you to see if you still possess the ability to dominate him. If you are able to maintain your domination, the horse may be quite happy to see that you have lost none of your strength and are still capable of looking after him. It is similar to the situation that arises when an insecure child tests the strength of his parent. When the child behaves badly it is often because of insecurity. The child is worried that the parents are not strong and are unable to cope with and protect him. The child actually wants to be disciplined because he wants evidence that his parents are strong. A horse's challenge to

authority is often based on a very similar psychology: he doesn't actually want to get away with it and wants to know that his dominator is still strong enough to look after him. Horses are great users of and believers in bluff, in the wild. In the domestic situation most handlers use bluff to keep their horses believing they are stronger and fiercer than their horses.

One of the most useful equine traits for the purpose of schooling is the horse's instinctive reliance on the hierarchical system. He subjugates his will to the will of the dominant horse. We can replace the dominant horse in this relationship and become the boss. We must instill some fear in the horse—show that we are capable of violence if he does not do as we wish. We do not actually have to hurt the horse to do this, because horses are so skillful in interpreting our body language. We adapt their body language, which fortunately is often similar to our own, to tell them we are superior. For example, if you were confident of your ability to handle the horse, you would walk confidently into the stable, with your head up and maintaining eye contact with the horse. You would not be nervous or hesitant when handling him (see chapter 4). Horses recognize this behavior as that of a dominant personality and most horses accept the domination without challenge. Whether he challenges or not largely depends on his natural bravery and confidence. If he does, you must be ready with an immediate confirmation of the threat you have previously been bluffing about. If, for example, a horse kicked you or bit you, or threatened to do either of these things, not only is it forgivable to smack him firmly: it is essential. You must deal with him as another horse would deal with him. He does not understand anything else. You must remain his boss otherwise he will become yours and you will be at his mercy. Horses who are allowed to become the boss can become dangerous and are always difficult to school.

VIOLENCE

Horses use violence or the threat of violence to establish their status among other horses. When horses meet for the first time, they must find out which one will be dominant. If one horse thinks of himself as the boss, he probably employs all the means at his disposal to convince the other

horse that he is the strongest and most courageous. He probably stands as tall as he can, with his head and neck elevated, so that he looks as big as possible. If this is enough to keep the other horse at a distance, it may be all that he needs to do to convince the other horse of his superiority—and there will be no violence. If the other horse also fancies his chances of being the boss, he also draws himself up to his full height, and the two horses probably approach each other. A squealing contest could then ensue, which may settle the matter—with the horse having the bravest, loudest squeal accepted as dominant. If this doesn't achieve a clear leader, the two may well fight. After one or all of these stages has been gone through, superiority becomes established, and they should resort to a peaceful coexistence.

Because of this possibility of fighting between newly introduced horses, one has to be vigilant when putting a new horse into a field with another horse or horses. If there is ever going to be a fight between them, it will be in the first day or two. After they have established who is to be the boss, they usually settle down and get on with each other very well. During these first few days you need to keep a careful eye on them. If you see the telltale signs of fighting, without putting yourself at risk, attempt to separate them. If possible, allow horses to meet for the first time over a fence, or preferably a hedge, so that they can decide on their ranking without hurting each other and without giving their owners heart attacks!

FLIGHT ANIMALS

Horses normally run away from pain or a threat of it. They do not normally confront the source of the pain. By and large this makes them easier to train, although sometimes this instinct to flee can make them behave oddly. One such circumstance is when the bit is hurting the horse's mouth. When the rider asks the horse to slow or stop, if the bit hurts, the horse may well run faster rather than slow down. Inevitably the rider will take a stronger hold on the bit, and the horse will run all the faster. He is running away from the pain and doesn't realize that he is making it worse for himself.

A horse will also run away from pain caused by an ill-fitting saddle.

Both of these situations could cause the horse to become out of the rider's control and hence very dangerous.

MEMORY

We must always remain aware of the superb memory of the horse. If he has suffered in particular circumstances, he will remember the suffering and the cause of it. It is very important to make learning experiences good experiences. When he does as we wish, we should make him feel good with a reward, like stopping work. We must also avoid bad experiences. If he is punished unfairly during schooling (particularly if he is a she), he will associate the punishment with what you are trying to teach him. It will probably mar this type of work for a very long time.

If we can give the horse good memories to associate with our training and handling, these will also stay for a long time. Good associations should be made with everything you do with your horse, if you want to make life easy and pleasant for both of you. Tacking up and grooming can be contrived to be good (or bad) experiences as can boxing, injecting and shoeing. It all depends on the way you handle him at these times and the pleasure that you can add to potentially unpleasant occasions. If he misbehaves because he is frightened or in pain, and you get cross with him or hit him, you will make this behavior even worse the next time. From thinking there might be something to be afraid of when, for example, you put the saddle on, now he is certain there is something to fear, because you added to and confirmed his fear by hurting him.

A horse's memory can be employed to advantage in other ways. Maybe we wish to teach an exercise—particularly, perhaps, a transition. If we ask the horse to do this at the same place in the arena each time, he will learn to expect it when he arrives there. This, however, can be both an advantage and a disad-

vantage. It can make the lesson easier to teach, but it can make the horse presume we want to perform at that point, whether or not we have actually asked him to. In other words, he learns to anticipate our commands. After he has learned the command, you should then ask him to perform it in different places at different times and insist that he doesn't make the transition himself without you specifically requesting it.

FREQUENT EXPOSURE

We have already come across the situation where a horse is frequently exposed to something that would normally be frightening; but that event was never followed by any pain or suffering, so eventually the horse will come to ignore it. This has obvious potential advantages. If the horse is frightened of traffic, then, from a safe distance, let him see a lot of it. Soon he will accept traffic as normal and non-threatening. If a horse is nervous when he goes to a show, take him to lots of shows until he realizes there is nothing to worry about. He will soon learn to relax. If he hates water, make him go into it a lot. He will soon learn there is nothing to fear from monsters of the deep. Police horses are repeatedly exposed to crowds and loud noises, unruly behavior and fire until they learn not to be frightened of them because they have not hurt them.

This exposure must be repeated many times during a relatively short period if the horse is to learn to ignore it. For example, if you want your horse to become accustomed to shows, you need to take him to a show every weekend for, say, five or six weeks. When he has become accustomed to

it, there is no need to visit shows regularly as he has learned that there is nothing to fear there. The same would be true of water. It would be of no use whatsoever forcing your horse through water just before a cross-country competition. He will remember the force but forget that there was nothing frightening in the water. If you took him through water virtually every day, preferably at different places for five or six days, he would realize and remember there was nothing in water that hurt him. Remember also to avoid punishment when trying to get him into water. He would remember the pain and associate it with the water, and that would make him even more frightened of water.

The same applies to many things that horses do not like doing. For example, going into and traveling in a horsebox or trailer. Get them in using the least possible force: take your time, reward them. When they are in, give them the best journey possible and make it short if you can. Just go around the block the first time, and very slowly. If they arrive back home after 10 minutes and it hasn't been too bad an experience for them, and if they do this again several times, they will learn and remember that traveling need hold no fears for them.

There are times, however, when this disregard of frequent exposure is counterproductive. For example, when a horse is not forward going, sometimes riders get into the habit of constantly kicking the horse. Initially the horse knows that to feel those legs on his sides means he must go faster. However, he becomes so used to feeling them, without anything unpleasant happening to him, that he learns to ignore them. You end up with a horse who has become unresponsive to the pressure of the legs on his side.

LEARNING BY ASSOCIATION

Horses are adept at learning by making associations. In their natural existence they use this for survival— for example, when they learn what is dangerous and to keep clear of it. The black dog has tried to bite him so in future he keeps away from it. He will learn this lesson very quickly. Learning by association teaches horses to respect the social order in the herd. If there is a horse that often kicks out when another horse goes behind it, the other horse will learn to respect this horse and not go too close to its back legs.

CHAPTER 3

How do we teach Horses?

Positive reinforcement is when we reward the horse for doing as we ask. For example, if we ride our horse at a jump and he jumps it, we could give him a reward such as a carrot, a pat or stopping work. Thus he learns that, if he does as he is told, he is rewarded. When he jumps it is pleasant for him because he gets a reward: he is learning to associate the jump with pleasure.

If, at the same time as giving him the carrot, you pat him and talk softly to him, he associates the pat and the voice with the reward. After a while the pat and the voice become a reward in themselves. This is secondary positive reinforcement.

Negative reinforcement is when the horse feels unpleasant sensations that go away when he does as you want. When you want the horse to stop or slow, you increase the contact and therefore the pressure on the horse's mouth. When he slows or stops, the pressure goes away. The horse has learned that if he feels pressure on his mouth, and he slows or stops, that pressure will go away. It is very important for the rider to know that the contact must be reduced when the horse does as he is told, otherwise the horse would become confused. The same is true of leg aids, whether they be given to drive the horse forwards or sideways. When the horse does as required, the increase of the leg aids must cease so that the horse knows he has done what was wanted.

Punishment is when the horse is subjected to an unpleasant sensation for doing what is wrong. This punishment is normally physical (i.e. pain, such as a smack from a whip, or by making the horse work hard), but it can come to be verbal. If, at the same time as hitting the horse, you shout at him, he will come to associate the verbal admonishment with the pain. Before long he feels just as punished by the raised voice as he does by the whip.

Frequent exposure (as discussed in chapter 2) is a method we use to accustom our horses to something they might otherwise find frightening. By seeing it or experiencing it frequently without any harm to themselves, they learn not to fear it.

Learning by association (as discussed in chapter 2) is a principle we use in many ways. Every time you put your legs on the sides of the horse, he associates it with going forwards. Suppose that at the same time you clicked your tongue. He would learn by association that every time you either clicked your tongue or put your legs on his side, he should go forwards. The same would be true when the horse learns to stop, or go more slowly, because he feels pressure on the bit. He associates pressure on the bit with going more slowly. Originally he learned this, and to move away from the leg, through negative reinforcement. As you can see, there can be more than one type of learning taking place at the same time.

TEACHING NEW THINGS

It is important to understand the learning process properly if you are intending to teach something new. When the horse was first ridden he knew absolutely nothing. Not that when the leg is put on he had to go forward, nor that when he felt more pressure from the bit in his mouth he had to stop or slow. He didn't even know that feeling pressure from the bit on one side of his mouth meant turn right or left. All these things had to be taught to him, slowly and painstakingly, little by little. Eventually the horse learned to associate the leg and rein aids with what the rider wanted.

When you ask your horse to do something that he has not done before, he probably won't understand what you want. Be prepared to show him, in as clear a way as possible, what you require of him. Do not presume that because you use the correct aids for a new maneuver or exercise, he will automatically comprehend what you want him to do. Everything has to be taught to him. He is not psychic. If someone hasn't already shown him what is required, you will have to. You will have to devise a method of teaching him, based

on the above and incorporating the correct aids. You will have to be patient: at first he won't have a clue about what you want him to do. Your aids will have to be very clear, and a little stronger than normal, so that there is no confusion for him. They must always be consistent, so that he learns to associate your aids with what you want him to do. The exercise must be repeated again and again until he has thoroughly learned his lesson.

ACCO FEEDS
213

ERRORS IN BEHAVIOR MANAGEMENT

Sometimes we inadvertently teach our horse to behave badly. For example, a horse tied up and left alone is often unhappy. He may therefore paw the ground or make a noise. His concerned owner comes to him to make sure that there is nothing wrong with him, or even to scold him for his behavior. The horse quickly realizes that, whenever he paws the ground, someone will come to him. Because he prefers to have someone with him, he continues pawing the ground or making a noise. He wants to keep someone coming to see him even if that person is cross with him. To a horse this is better than being alone. The moral of this story is: do not go and see him when he does this (unless you really do think he is putting himself in danger).

Be careful with punishment as a training method. You must be sure that the horse has been naughty rather than confused. Punishment must be administered immediately after the wrongdoing. The horse must know that the punishment is the consequence of his behavior. If there is a delay, and for this reason or

any other reason the horse is unsure why he is being punished, it will produce confusion, and probably even worse behavior.

It is also important that the horse does not associate his punishment with the work he is doing. If, for example, he refused several jumps and was smacked for each refusal, he would probably associate being smacked with jumping. He may always hate jumping as a result. If the horse is difficult about jumping, it is essential to find another way that is not unpleasant. Perhaps you could start with smaller jumps, praising and rewarding him every time he jumped. This would replace punishment with reward or positive reinforcement, which is always a step in the right direction!

CHAPTER 4

How do horses Communicate?

I think it must be almost every horse owner's dream to have a horse that can talk—one's own "Mr. Ed," for those of us old enough to remember TV's talking horse! What most don't realize is that horses do talk to us in many ways. They have a very varied system of communication, based largely on body language, which can help us understand what they are trying to communicate. If we can learn this language, we can communicate with them by the same system. Good communication leads to a better understanding of each other's needs and to an improved relationship.

Because horses are such social beings, communication between themselves and other members of their group is very important to them. It is a vital factor in organizing and maintaining the social cohesion that is essential for their survival.

HOW DO HORSES COMMUNICATE WITH EACH OTHER?

By sound

The nicker

This is a low, soft sound that is usually associated with pleasure, either experienced or anticipated, by the horse. A mare would nicker on being reunited with her foal, as would the

hungry horse when his owner appears bearing food, or the lonely horse when company approaches. The horse is saying, "This is good; I'm happy."

The whinny

This is used to tell other horses where the whinnying horse is, and asks them to respond by whinnying so that their location can be judged. It means, "I'm here—

where are you?" It is high-pitched and travels well over distance. Horses are skilled at judging the direction from which the sound has come. When grazing, horses normally keep other members of their group in sight. They, therefore, tend to rely more on visual signals than on sound. When horses are out of sight of each other, audible signals replace visual ones. This is why stabled horses often call if they are unable to see each other. It is not necessarily a sound of distress, often only a communication. You can tell from the pitch of the whinny when it becomes a sound of distress. It becomes higher and louder. Some horses are particularly unhappy if they are on their own. If they are able to communicate with another horse, but unable to be with him, they will become even more distressed.

The hard blow or snort.

This is a sound produced when there is something that is potentially frightening or interesting about. The animal who has made it often turns and stares at whatever has caught his attention before, during and after he makes the sound. It is a loud noise and commands the attention of the other horses. The snorting horse is almost saying, "Have you seen this? I don't like the look of it—be careful."

The squeal

This sound is often made when two horses meet. They approach, cautiously touch noses and one or the other of them may squeal, or perhaps both of them squeal. When they touch noses they are sizing each other up. The squeal is a challenge to the other horse. The squealing horse is saying he is the boss. It is often enough to establish him as the dominant horse, provided that the other horse accepts this situation. If he doesn't squeal, he accepts the first horse as the dominant one.

If the second horse does squeal, it means he is not happy to accept the first horse as his superior. At this stage the horse with the loudest squeal may win the contest. In the animal kingdom, he who can make the loudest noise is often the largest and most dangerous, and therefore the one to be respected. It is a little bit like two small boys in the playground, trying to face each other off before a fight. Their voices will gradually rise until they are shouting, because the volume of the voice makes promise of a stronger person. In the same way, the horse making the larger noise asserts that he is stronger. If this is not sufficient to settle the matter, the conversation may turn into a fight between the two horses. Neither admits to being the lesser, and physical strength will have to win the day. Not all horses meeting in this way squeal. Sometimes they merely introduce themselves to each other and are happy with each other's existing status. They walk away without making a sound.

We know the approximate meaning of this communication, but it doesn't seem to have any bearing on our relationship with horses. They never seem to squeal at us, and I've never yet heard a human squeal at a horse! The volume of the sound, however, is of significance. Because horses respect those who make loud noises, a human whose voice is loud is far more likely to instill fear and respect into a horse. Shouting at a badly behaved horse is something humans already do automatically. It is a behavior we use with each other, so we naturally extend it to our communication with the horse. Similarly, when we wish to be friends with the horse, we speak in a quiet voice. Often men are more respected by horses than women. In part this is because men tend to have deeper and louder voices.

The soft blow

This sounds as if the horse is blowing his nose. Unlike the hard blow or snort, it means that the horse is relaxed. You wouldn't hear a tense horse making this noise. When you are riding, it is good to hear this sound from him, because it means you are not stressing him and he is ready to begin work. When he blows like this, he is pushing air out of his lungs, showing that they are not tense and are able to work to their maximum.

DO THEY UNDERSTAND THE MEANING OF NOISES OTHER HORSES MAKE?

Of course. There would be no point in making different sounds unless other horses knew why they were making them and that someone else would understand them.

DO THEY UNDERSTAND THE SOUNDS HUMANS MAKE?

No. They cannot recognize words but they can associate certain types of sound with the circumstances in which they heard them. For example, a sharp sound, such as "no" when the animal is naughty, may often have been accompanied by a smack. Very quickly, the horse associates "no", said in a harsh way, as a reprimand. When we speak softly to a horse, and stroke it gently at the same time, the horse learns to associate a soft voice with pleasant circumstances. When we are training a horse, "walk on" said in a commanding way is associated with the dominant status of the trainer. The words themselves are probably not recognized as such, but the feeling behind the words, the tone, the pitch and the combination of pitches is communicated to the horse because of the associations he has with them. For example "walk on" is probably said in two pitches, "walk" being high, "on" being lower, and the "n" being held for a moment longer. It becomes almost musical, and, if repeated in the same way every time that you require the horse to "walk on," he will recognize the command. When you ask the horse to "trot" you will often say this as "terrrrrot". Again, if this sound is repeated when trot is required, it will be recognized. So, if you wish to train your horse by sound, use the same sound and the same intonation or sets of intonations. Accompany the sound by the same actions which

ask him to perform the task you require. Repeated often enough, the horse gets to know what you want, merely by recognizing what he has heard.

By smell

Horses have a very well developed sense of smell and use it to assess their environment. As for using it for communication, this is probably limited to leaving their droppings for others to know that they have been there.

By behavior

Sometimes horses give very obvious clues as to their feelings and what they wish to communicate to others, for example:

Swishing tail–He is telling you he is unhappy. It could be a fly or the rider is annoying him.

Flattened ears–"Beware! I'm going to attack you if you don't do as I wish."

Touching noses–"Hello" or "Hello, who are you?" or "I like you."

Head held low–"I'm not going to hurt you. In fact, I'm probably not here."

Keeping the side of the body facing another animal–"I am very insignificant. I pose no threat to you. I am definitely not here."

Facing another horse with eyes or body–"I am very brave, very superior and not the least bit frightened of you. Do you want to take me on, or are you going to do as I wish?"

A high head carriage–"I'm better than everyone here so don't mess with me."

Quarters angled or turned toward another–"If you don't get out of the way I'll kick you."

Bared teeth–"Go away or I'll bite you."

Clapping the mouth or chewing– "I admit it. You're the boss. I'm nobody. Will you be my friend?"

Pawing the ground–"I'm not too happy" or "I'm going to roll here."

Looking back–Horses who expect to be followed often look back at those they wish to come with them, before they walk on.

Horses also give relatively subtle clues as to their personality or feelings.

No eye contact–"I'm a little afraid of you. If I don't look at you perhaps you won't look at me. Perhaps you won't realize I'm here."

Eye contact is used for communication and tells us what mood the horse is in:

Soft eyes–relaxed happy horse.

Wild eyes with the white showing–frightened horse.

Angry eyes, pleading eyes–Other horses will easily pick up on these facial expressions just as we pick up on the look on another person's face. Horses have very expressive faces –sad, contented, quizzical, frightened, frightening or disdainful. We can interpret their facial expressions just as we can with humans. If horses can interpret the facial expressions of other horses, and these are similar to our own, it is possible that they may be able to understand human facial expressions too.

Flared nostrils–They show fear or anger and are associated with the requirement for more oxygen needed for either a fight or a flight.

HOW DO HORSES LISTEN?

They will face in the direction, in which they are listening. They also face their ears in the direction of what they are looking at or concentrating on. It feels as if they are looking at you with their ears. In fact, their peripheral vision is so good that they can see you, even when their head is not turned towards you. By turning their ears towards you they are concentrating their hearing in your direction. When you are riding, if both of the horse's ears are turned back towards you, the horse is concentrating on his work and on what you are telling him to do. He is listening to you, even though you have not made a single noise: your communications have all been physical ones. You then know that you have his attention and concentration.

CAN A HORSE TELL YOU WHAT IS WRONG WITH HIM?

You need to build up a catalogue of his characteristics of behavior. This helps you to understand his symptoms and make an accurate or a fairly accurate diagnosis. For example: kicking stomach, and/or walking round box looking at stomach, and/or rolling agitatedly will probably be some type of colic; head hanging low, or not eating, or a temperature—a virus?

Be alert to changes in your horse's behavior. Remember what has happened in the past to this horse or other horses. Look at the whole horse or feel him under you when he is well. Make a note of it so you can tell the difference when he is not. Make yourself sensitive to his moods, his behavior and his movement. Then you will be more able to pick up on anything that is wrong, and you will know when things are not going well and the horse is unhappy.

Particularly notice how your horse greets you, either in the field or the stable. If he normally has his head over the door and greets you with a whinny, you should worry about him if he remains standing in a corner. Similarly, if your horse usually looks up when you call him in the field, and this time he ignores you, perhaps he might have a problem: investigate.

OUR COMMUNICATION SYSTEM: THE AIDS

Riders have created the aids as a method of communicating with horses. Each horse has to be taught what these aids mean. He is not possessed of this knowledge at birth. In creating them we have tried to use sensory signals that are easily understood by the horse.

The aids are given using our hands via the reins, our legs, our backs, our balance and occasionally our voices. It is possible to teach horses to respond to other methods of communication. For example, you could teach a horse to canter by pressing with your finger on the right side of the withers for right canter and on the left for left canter. For now, however, we will concentrate on the established aids.

Most of the aids are as they are for obvious practical reasons. For example, when you wish a horse to go to the right, you ask it with the right rein to bring its head to the right, and then the rest of the horse follows. It is easy for us and for the horse to understand. If we wish him to move the whole of his body to the right, we push with our left leg. Again, it is easy for both the horse and ourselves to understand. It is almost the same as getting off the horse and physically pushing him from his left side, so that his whole body moves to the right.

Some of the aids use the laws of physics to help the horse understand what is required, but in each there is an element of association. When he

has learned the meaning of the aid in this way, it will not be long before he does what is required merely because he feels the aid and knows what it means, rather than waiting for the physical force of the aid. For example, if you wish to turn right and shorten the rein on that side by the smallest amount, he will happily go to the right. You do not have to pull his head over with the right rein as you might have done when he was first ridden. He is doing it because he knows what it means, not because you are forcing him. Gradually you can reduce, and then reduce again, the strength of the aid because the horse still understands what you want of him. The less physical the aid, the less disturbance you cause to the balance and harmony of the horse's movements.

We have to beware of giving the horse signals unconsciously when we do not intend to. He is so adept at picking up on associations. Remember the examples given earlier. He appears to anticipate what we want him to do, because we are doing things we are unaware of, like changing our position and shortening the rein before we canter. Keep your body still, until you actually apply the aid.

Horses can understand the body language of other horses and may interpret our body language in their own terms. A lowered extended arm looks much like the horse's lowered head, meaning submission or cessation of confrontation. Facing horses frontally is confrontational, whereas the side of our body is not confrontational. If you walk towards a horse, looking into his eyes and facing his body with yours, he regards you as dominant and probably submits to you. If, however, you walked into the stable quietly, with your head down and your body at less than its full height, the horse would know that you were timid and he would probably be able to boss you around. If, every time he moved his quarters in your direction, you leaped away expecting him to kick, he would recognize your nervousness and take advantage of it. Hence a confident, upstanding and/or tall person who is striding out is someone to be reckoned with. A person with a lowered head and small steps is someone who can be bossed. A tall person could dominate a horse naturally, while a shorter individual has to prove he is not frightened, because instinctively the horse presumes the smaller person to be less strong. A horse regards a person who speaks with a strong voice as someone to be wary of. If we feel confident with horses, it shows in the way we behave and they will know who we are. The horse assesses you as you assess yourself.

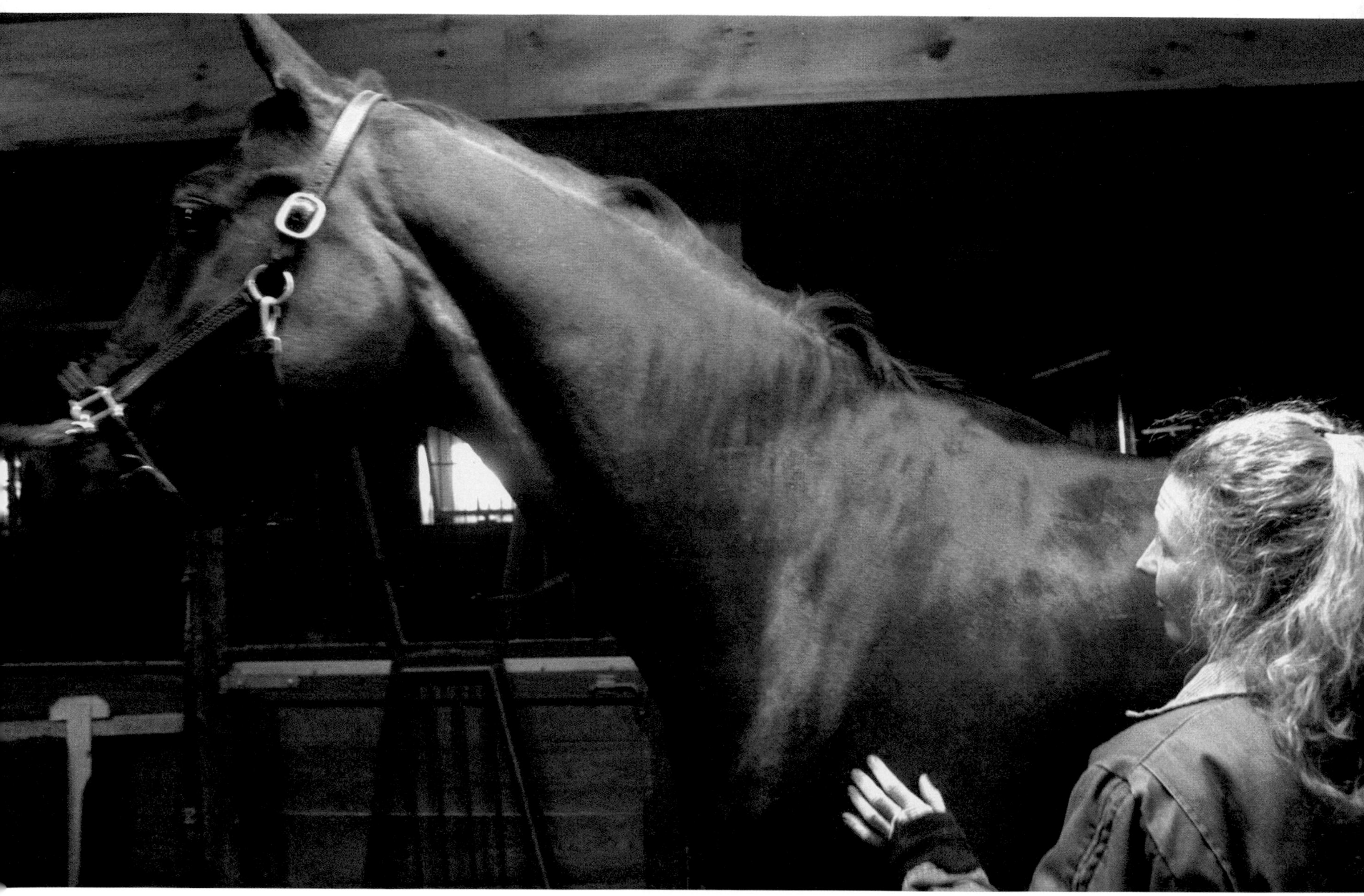

48

CHAPTER 5

Dominating your Horse

If we are to manage horses effectively, we must persuade them that we are their superiors. There must be no question in their minds about this. Though we must treat them fairly, and kindly, this kindness must not extend to softness if you are faced with bad behavior or disobedience. When you require them to do something, if you know they understand what you require and you know they are capable of achieving it, then you must insist that they do it. This does not mean you should be cruel to them in any way; it merely means that you must not let them get away with any disobedience. If a horse thinks that a rider will tolerate disobedience, this is one of the biggest obstacles to success.

Disciplining horses begins long before you get on their backs. It starts with the way you handle your horse the very first time you meet him, and how you continue from then on. The way you handle him includes the way you walk up to him, how you hold your body, how you look at him and how you touch him. The way you stand and walk, the way you speak to him, the way you groom him, pick his feet out, tack him up, lead him, ride him and most particularly the way in which you deal with naughtiness. You must be confident with him at all times (see chapter 3). He must know from the way you handle yourself that you are his boss and are not at all frightened of him.

If he seeks to challenge this domination, you must leave him in no doubt that you will not tolerate any challenges! The way in which the horse challenges you will determine the way in which you meet his challenge. When meeting his challenge or his naughtiness, the punishment should fit the crime: if he has tried to, threatened to, or succeeded in kicking or biting you, a very firm whack would fit the bill. If the misdemeanor is less, the punishment also should be less.

Needless to say, all this behavior on our part is pure bluff. There is no chance that we could physically overpower a horse or make him do as we wish by forcing him. We are playacting when we are with horses—pretending we are huge and powerful. The way we relate to him must always convince the horse that this is the case. If he ever discovers that it is a bluff, and that he is in fact much stronger, it may become almost impossible to school him.

THE WAY YOU LOOK AT YOUR HORSE

A subordinate horse would not look a dominant horse directly in the eye for any length of time: this would provoke a confrontation. The more cowardly of the two will avoid this, because he doesn't want the battle. The dominant horse, however, will look the other in the eye because he knows he is boss. Nervous and gentle humans also tend to avoid direct eye contact with other humans, as well as with horses. No wonder horses are so quick to work out which humans are capable of dominating them—innately we use much of the same body language. If you are to be the dominant one in the relationship you must look your horse directly in the eye.

THE WAY YOU TURN YOUR BODY

If one horse faces another horse with the whole of the front of his body, it is potentially confrontational, just like direct, maintained eye contact. Imagine a subservient horse creeping past a dominant horse. He keeps the side of his body towards the dominant horse and only looks at him from the corner of his eye. It is as if he can hardly see the dominant horse and is hoping the dominant horse will

hardly notice him either. The position of his body makes no confrontation to the other horse, so he is happily ignored. By walking past him in this manner he is saying, "I am unimportant. I will not be a threat to you; just ignore me."

Imagine a more confident horse who, unafraid of a battle, walks straight up to the other horse face to face, eye to eye. At this point there is either a confrontation, and perhaps a fight, or one of the horses will back down. Most likely the latter.

So, if you turn and face your horse and look him in the eye, he knows you are somebody who is not afraid to confront him. You are in the running to be the boss.

THE WAY YOU STAND

The subservient horse mentioned above probably sidles past the other horse with his head close to the ground. This is to make himself look smaller. The smaller you are the less threatening you are. Imagine the dominant horse standing, looking at the subservient horse, or perhaps the dominant stallion warding off all comers: he stands as tall as he can make himself, his neck arched and his head high. He wants to look as big as he can, and threatening.

If you want to impress your horse, make yourself appear as big as possible—don't creep past him ignominiously. Take confident strides around him and walk towards him confidently: he will recognize you as a powerful being. If he backs off that is fine. He is a little fearful of you; you are well on the road to being the boss.

THE WAY YOU SPEAK

When two horses confront each other, the next stage of the meeting may be a squealing competition. The squeal is one of the loudest noises a horse makes. The horse who makes the loudest squeal may be accepted as the victor in the battle for dominance. We humans don't enter into the squealing contest, but we can assert our superiority by speaking with a strong voice when we wish the horse to recognize us as the dominant partner. Conversely, if we wish to be his friend, we can speak softly.

It is worth noting at this point the reasons why men often manage to win the respect of horses where a woman fails. Consider the (usually) greater physical strength of a man, his greater size and deeper, louder voice. This is more respected

by the horse, who has learned from experience that the larger and noisier the potential threat, the more dangerous it is likely to be. It could also be that women tend to be gentler and kinder to horses, which is a trait that the horse would recognize as a weakness.

Once having won respect from the horse, you will find him all the more eager to bond and become your friend. The horse recognizes that having such a powerful person for a friend is very much to his advantage. He will be appreciative of the love and care you show him. This combination of power and affection creates the strongest bond possible.

THE WAY YOU HANDLE HIM

This is when the horse really weighs you up as a character. How do you touch him? How do you brush him? If your handling of him is confident and easy, not nervous and hesitant, he knows you do not fear him, and, therefore, perhaps he may treat you with caution.

If, on the other hand, you are nervous, tense and perhaps over gentle, he suspects that he can push you around. Few horses can resist the temptation of taking a nervous person for a ride—figuratively speaking of course!

THE WAY YOU MANAGE HIS NAUGHTINESS

There are very, very few saintly horses who never bite, kick, paw the ground or mess about. The vast majority challenge your authority at some time. They are testing the ground to see how you will respond. If you do nothing, or little, they will probably take it a little further and be a little naughtier. Before you know where you are, you could have a thoroughly badly behaved horse on your hands and not because the horse is bad, but because you are useless at teaching him how to respect you.

There is, sadly, only one way that I know of to deal with bad behavior: just as the mother would reprimand her foal when he steps out of line, you must reprimand your charge when he misbehaves. A small smack will be ignored; it must be sufficiently hard for the horse not to wish to invite a recurrence of the punishment by misbehaving again. A firm smack will be respected. Anything much more than this will have a detrimental effect on your relation-

ship, and it is to be abhorred if it reflects violence or cruelty in any way. If you have to smack your horse, avoid doing this on his head. Because of the eyes and the delicate tissue of the head, it is easy to physically damage your horse by hitting him here and even easier to create a head shy horse. (A head shy horse is one who nervously lifts his head into the air every time you lift your hand towards it.) A punishment must be administered immediately so that the horse can relate it to his wrongdoing. If there is any kind of gap, it will cause the horse a lot of confusion and upset, for he will not remember what it was for. The shoulders, the neck, the quarters and behind the girth are normal areas to administer punishment. Where you will administer it will depend on your location in relation to the horse at the time of the misdemeanor. You can smack with your open hand as it creates a lot of noise; but beware, it can hurt you a good deal more than it does the horse. A riding stick or whip, used once, is often more effective.

It is difficult to say exactly where or with what you should discipline your horse. It is something that has

to be done immediately and therefore the part of the horse that is nearest at the time is the most available. Preferably it would also involve that part of the horse that has committed the offense. This will help him understand what the punishment is for. It is unwise to hit your horse if standing behind him. He may decide to retaliate and you would be in a very vulnerable position. If you were holding a riding stick, you would use that, or if you were not, you use your hand. Do not

lose the moment by going to get a stick. The horse may forget the connection between the crime and the punishment and will regard your behavior as cold-blooded.

When you smack your horse, discipline him with your voice at the same time. If you always do this, after a while you will only need to shout at him and it will be sufficient to make him feel suitably punished. Some horses are sensitive and will not need a physical reprimand. A verbal admonishment will be all they need to understand that you are displeased with them. Anything more would be cruel and probably make them frightened and tense.

Sometimes the bad behavior occurs when the horse is being ridden—for example, a rear or a buck. This is difficult to deal with. You know that, if you smack your horse, you are probably inviting more of the same from him. You are, quite justifiably, frightened of being hurt if he throws you off. Instead of smacking your horse, you could try riding him forwards very strongly. If he obeys your leg and goes forwards, you have won the argument. If he disobeys your leg and repeats the buck or rear, you must punish your horse. A firm smack behind the leg with the riding stick will let him know you are not happy with him. He will probably buck or rear again and you will have to smack him again. At this point most horses give up and start to behave themselves. Enforcing horse discipline may well test your riding ability, and certainly your nerve, but, thankfully, once you have established yourself as his boss, your horse will misbehave less and less frequently. When your horse has done as you asked him, be sure to remember to praise him—give him every reason to behave well.

Most horses give up when they recognize you are not going to be bullied or frightened by them. It is down to your bravery, and whether you mind the possibility of falling off. The problem with not taking that risk is that the horse will know that he is boss. You are frightened of him and he can do what he likes. At this point, some people send their horse away for schooling (to someone who is not afraid). Unfortunately, the problem is a personal one between you and your horse. Another person may well be able to stop him bucking or rearing, but when the horse comes home he recognizes you and remembers that you were the coward who didn't stand up to him. If this is your case, perhaps you would be better selling this horse and buying a more amenable animal.

When chastising the horse, the voice should be used at the same time as any other form of reprimand. If this is done every time the horse needs discipline, he will associate the voice with punishment. The voice may ultimately suffice on its own as a punishment, without the need for anything more.

The playacting described above is not necessarily forever. When you have established your relationship, and he knows you are dominant, you can normally relax into a gentler way of living with each other without the need to be constantly asserting your supremacy. Occasionally, though, the horse (depending on his character) may seek an opportunity to test this—just be ready to deal with it as before.

MORE SERIOUS BAD BEHAVIOR

Some people say that bad horses are made, not born. Usually this is true, but there are some horses, though thankfully precious few, who are born determined to be the boss. They seek to establish their dominance in the way that they would in the herd—by violence. They will kick and bite, rear and buck in an attempt to boss you. This would be fine if they were being left out in the field and never ridden. But it is unacceptable if, every time you want to ride them, they again try to reestablish their dominance—by not letting you catch them, by rearing, biting or kicking. Thankfully there really are very few animals who are like this naturally, but it is easy for horses like this to be created through their owner's mishandling. If you have a horse who manifests these tendencies, there is only one way forward. That is, to be prepared to prove to him that you can dominate him.

A word of warning: do not attempt to handle really violent horses unless you are very experienced, competent and confident with horses. Some (though very, very few) can be mean, nasty and potentially dangerous. In these circumstances the trainer assumes a role similar to that of a lion tamer! It is a dangerous job and one for a professional who has nerves of steel and knows exactly what he is doing.

If your horse bites or kicks you, or threatens to do either of these things, there is rarely any choice for you but to smack him. This is the language of the herd. You are telling him you are not afraid of him and if he hurts you, or tries to, you will hurt him more. It seems awful that a book, whose ethos is one of gentleness, love and kindness to the horse, recommends hitting them, but now you are talking horse language. This is how they seek dominance in the herd and it is how you must establish dominance now. You must have an ultimate punishment available to use on a badly behaved horse. There has to be a reason for the horse to do as he is told.

If you are nervous you have a problem. You must become an actor. Pretend to be confident. Follow all the rules set out for convincing your horse that you are the boss. However, it may be that the horse has already evaluated your personality and knows he can intimidate you. It is, therefore, doubly difficult for you to convince him that your character and confidence have changed overnight; but this is what you must do. The best way to do it is to shell-shock him into believing you have changed, by making yourself very theatrically dominant. Everything you do must be over-the-top. Make a lot of noise when you go into the stable. If the horse puts a foot out of line, be very, very firm with him. You must become so utterly dominant that he will believe you really have changed. After you have convinced him, and his behavior starts to improve, you can re-

duce the playacting, but you must never stop it altogether. If you were to slip back into the same intimidated person as before, he will quickly realize and start to take advantage again. He will value you as you value yourself—that is, as his subordinate.

There is often a metamorphosis when a badly behaved horse is sent away for schooling. He arrives at the trainer's yard and is instantly better behaved. The reason is that the horse is phased by the new surroundings and people. At first he tries to work out where he belongs in the hierarchy and behaves well, at least until he has worked out whom, if anyone, he can boss around and whom he can't. The people there are professionals and not the least bit intimidated by him. He knows this from their body language and how they handle him. Throughout his time there he will behave because they are dominant, and he has to do as he is told. When his schooling has finished, he is returned to his owner a changed horse—for about two days. It won't be long before the horse remembers his old owner and behaves just as he did before. The moral of this story: perhaps it is the owner who should go away for schooling!

You may think that being so firm with your horse is cruel, but it is the opposite. Once your horse knows you are the boss, he relaxes in your company. He finds strength in your strength and this makes him secure and happy. Just like children, horses need discipline, without which they would be unhappy, difficult creatures. Remember that to be a successful rider, just as to be a successful parent, you need to be strong enough to be firm. True affection from your horse is engendered from the knowledge that he is secure in your strong but caring company. Animals roaming freely in the wild attach themselves to a strong friend—and in exactly the same way your horse will attach himself to you, because he perceives that you will fend off all attackers and look after him. The fact that you feed him as well, and are kind to him when he is good, serves to reinforce this dependency and the desire to keep you as his friend by doing as you ask.

CHAPTER 6

REWARD OR PUNISHMENT?

POSITIVE REINFORCEMENT

Traditionally, the attitude of the horse training industry is, if the horse does as he is asked, everything is fine. If he doesn't, he will be punished. In other words, horses are trained by punishment or fear. The whip is often to hand and we expect horses to be scared of it.

The alternative method of training is by positive reinforcement. The horse is praised when he does things correctly, and given a reward. The advantage of positive reinforcement is that, because pleasant things happen during training sessions, the whole atmosphere changes. Instead of being filled with dread, it becomes a happy time that the horse can look forward to. Both horse and rider share this benevolent feeling and, because the horse is enjoying his work, he should perform better.

The rewards you can give your horse vary. You might give him a rest, or stroke his neck. Stopping work altogether is the greatest reward. You can also praise him with your voice. Some are against it, but giving the horse a tidbit is easily understood and welcome as a reward, though there are potential problems. The horse may come to expect to be given something. He could develop bad habits such as stopping of his own accord or, when stopped, reach towards your hand with his mouth. Some horses are particularly prone to this but your horse can be trained to wait for you to offer the reward rather than demand it. Simply use the aid to go on a little more assertively, when he is thinking about stopping. Keep a firm hold on the reins if he begins to reach towards you. This should be adequate to convey your intention to him.

This morning my very mischievous kitten was up to high jinks in the bedroom. I was going out, so, before I could put the alarm on, I had to put the kitten out. The morning before, I had been in the same situation and tried to chase him out of the room. He had darted everywhere and it took me several minutes before I finally got him out. The result: a defeated, unhappy cat and a tired me. This morning, another approach. Walking out of the room I called "puss, puss," in very much the same kind of voice as I would use to tell him there was food being served. The kitten, anticipating something nice, followed me out immediately. The moral of the story: always try to get your way without a fight, and try to keep the ending happy!

If you use these kinds of technique with your horse, life is much easier and more pleasant. Don't meet him head on, waiting for a fight. Use your brain and find the easy way

round. Look for the best way to teach something. Last year a friend told me her horse became quite silly every time she asked it to do half pass. He should have found this maneuver quite easy, but he didn't and got distressed when asked for it. She could have carried on asking him to do it, using stronger and stronger aids, but this would probably have made him more upset. Instead, she went back to a very similar but easier exercise—leg yielding. The horse had no problem with this so she

asked him to do this exercise during every schooling session. When she was sure he was relaxed and happy with leg yielding, she slightly changed the angle of his body bit by bit, until he was doing half pass without any fuss or worry.

THE PRINCIPLES OF LEARNING

Some of the answers you seek may be found in this section, but there can never be a comprehensive guide on how to do it. There is too wide a variety of situations and too many difficult kinds of horse. It is up to you to use your brains all the time to work out the best solution.

When your horse has worked for you, and given more then he has before, make a big fuss of him and perhaps stop work. He will know this is a reward and horses have such good memories that he will not forget. Fill his mind full with good associations and memories when he does well for you. Soon he will learn that pleasing you is one of the best things in the world. It is wonderful when, every time you take him out and train him, he regards it as a treat.

PUNISHMENT

Occasionally you have to administer discipline or punishment. There are invariably times when he misbehaves or is disobedient. Minimize these occasions and keep the relationship between the two of you sweet. Don't ever let a schooling session finish on a bad note. If your horse has been really uncooperative and difficult, ask him to do something you know he will do well, and then praise or reward him. Either do this again or find something else he will do well. Again praise or reward him. Finish the lesson there. If he has done as he is told, and felt good about it, he will remember this the next time you school him. Get him into the habit of always doing as he is told and always feeling good about it because he has been rewarded. As long as you do not ask him to do anything that is difficult for him, and proceed slowly with his training, you need never stray far from this philosophy.

There are other times when you can use positive reinforcement as a training aid. Imagine the horse who hates having his girth tightened. The horse may snap at you, or flinch, or lift a leg in half threat. Naughty though this behavior is, the horse does it because of hatred or fear of the tightened girth. If we now get angry and smack him, or shout at him if he registers his displeasure, his dislike or fear is reinforced because of your scolding.

Instead of being cross, try to understand how he feels. Just before and while you tighten the girth, stroke your horse and talk to him nicely. Perhaps give him a tidbit. Try to help him forget about the discomfort of the girth and only think about the pleasant things that are happening to him. If you repeat this every time the girth is tightened, eventually he should associate it with desirable sensations. Ultimately you should be able to make less and less fuss of him as his dislike for the girth is tempered. You have put a happy association in the place of an unpleasant experience.

ON THE ROAD

Some horses have a nervous disposition. Some situations make them even more nervous and tense: for example, riding out on the road. Obviously this makes them unsafe in traffic. Because they are nervous, they misbehave—jumping out from things in the hedge or swinging their quarters into the path of vehicles. Then the rider often gets nervous too, and may often get cross with the horse. It sounds like stating the obvious, but, if you get cross with a nervous horse, all you get is a more nervous and badly behaved horse. A calm rider does far more for this type of horse. If you can give the horse something else to think about while he is on the road, you may be able to take his mind off what is upsetting him. A series of transitions—walk, trot, walk, halt, trot, etc.—are very useful. Riding your horse along the right-hand side of the road, turn his head very slightly to the left. To stop him from walking into the road, keep your left leg against his side and a firm contact on your right rein. This keeps him mentally occupied, and in a safe outline when traffic is approaching. When the horse's head is turned a little to the left, his left eye can see behind him. Traffic coming up behind him is seen with this eye. If it frightens him, this makes him move away from it, safely towards the road's verge. If he sees the traffic coming from the rear with his right eye, he will move away from it to the left, which takes him out into the middle of the road. When the traffic does pass by, talk to him in a calm reassuring voice.

When you are riding, avoid tension in your own body. If you are nervous, the horse will pick up on it. If you are frightened, he will think there is reason for him to be frightened also. Relax your body so as to let him know you are not nervous (even if you are). This helps him to relax because he feels the relaxation in your body. If you find it difficult to relax, sing a song to yourself.

If you are riding past something that makes the horse nervous, do not make him look at it. This only makes him become more nervous. Keep his head away from it. Try and pretend that it doesn't exist or, even if it does, it is nothing to make a fuss about. There is a good chance the horse will believe you.

Use a horse's reaction to frequent exposure to make him better behaved on the road. Taking horses out every day for a week, using the same stretch of road, should make them less nervous of what they encounter there. If a horse has been frightened of something he hears or sees in the roadside, but is never hurt by it, he learns to ignore it. If, however, the rider scolds the horse when he jumps away in fright, then by hurting his horse, the rider has reinforced his horse's fear. The horse feels justified in being frightened of what is in the roadside because, as an indirect result of it, he has felt pain.

DON'T REWARD BAD BEHAVIOR

You may be teaching your horse a new or difficult exercise when he becomes nervous and tense. It could be that he is struggling to cope with understanding or performing what you want. Often, when the horse gets tense and disobedient, the rider gets cross and the horse gets even tenser. This is counterproductive. It creates a bad memory for the horse, which is linked to this particular work. Try to keep calm and think of another easier way to teach the lesson. The horse should also remain calm and learn the lesson with no bad associations. It may take a little longer than you had hoped, but the benefits are many.

There are times when you take your horse out to train him and he is badly behaved. He will not settle to work, or will not do as you ask him. It could be because the horse is tense, but, whatever the reason, it is a bad idea to stop work because of this. If you do, you are teaching him to associate being bad with earning a rest and reward. No matter how badly he behaves (and very often it can seem pointless carrying on), you must keep going. You know your horse. Find something he likes to do, or does easily. Do this until his behavior improves, then give him a rest or a reward. If it doesn't improve, don't give him the reward he expects. For example, suppose that after work he usually goes out with the other horses. Instead of this, put him on his own in the stable, or don't give him hay and a feed. Later bring him out and ride him some more. Again, do something he will find easy. Don't confront him. This time you hope he will do something that is worthy of praise. Seize on this, make a fuss of him, and give him his reward. He must never be given a reward for bad behavior, only for good. Keep on with this system until the penny drops.

NAUGHTINESS?

One of the most difficult problems one is confronted with when schooling horses is disobedience. Is the horse being naughty, or doesn't he understand what you have asked him to do? Perhaps he is physically incapable of performing the task, or finds it physically difficult. Perhaps the horse has become tense and this makes him unable to settle down to his work. To know how to deal with his disobedience, you

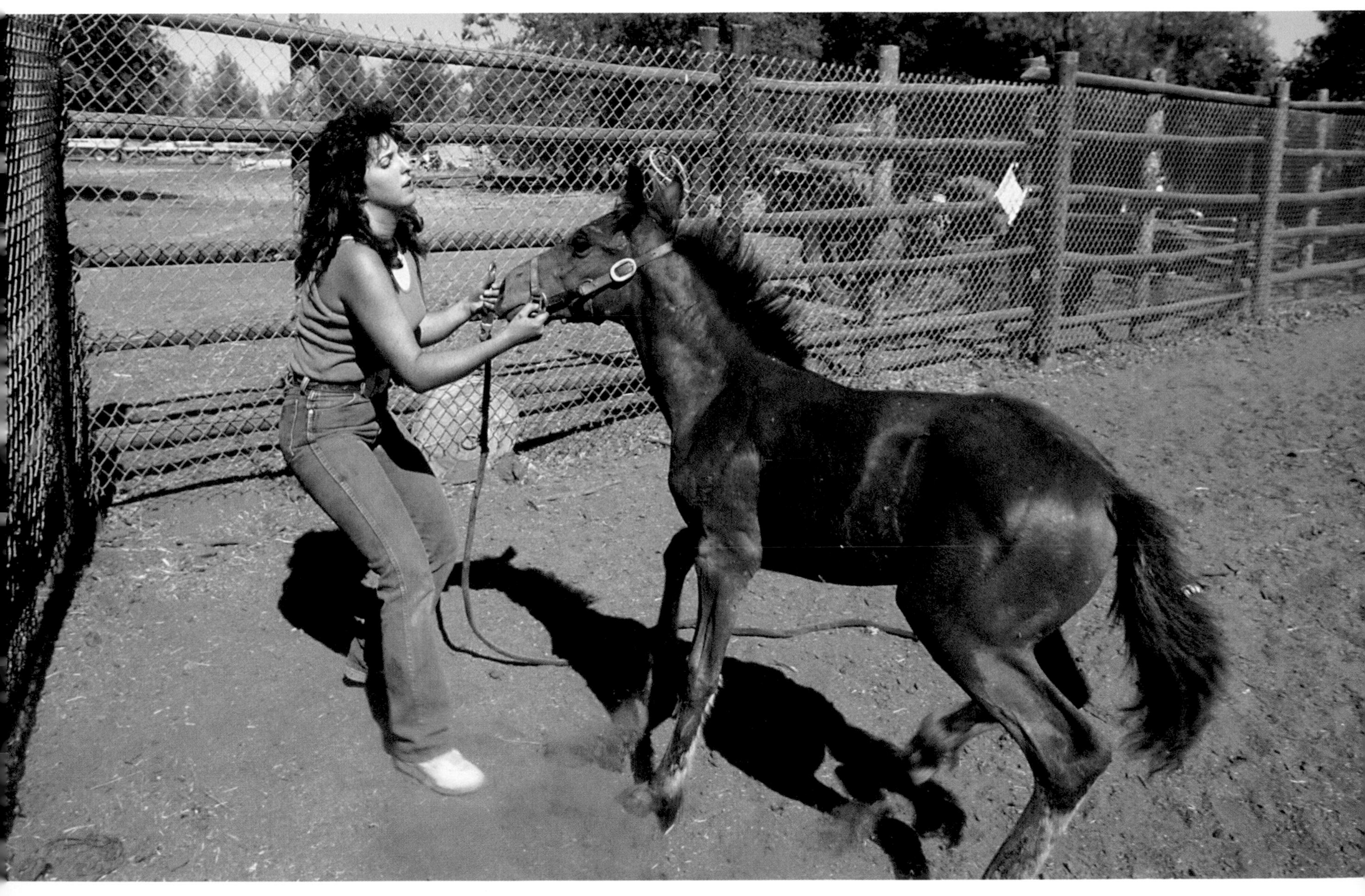

need to know the reason for it. If you are totally sure he is being naughty, it isn't a problem. If he were being demonstrably naughty—bucking, rearing or kicking—a smack would be in order. Smacking a nervous horse, though, even if he has appeared naughty, is always counterproductive. It makes him even more nervous. He may not recover during that schooling session. You need to know why he is behaving as he is. If he is merely not doing as you ask, repeat the request until he does it.

Some horses, particularly intelligent mares, resent being disciplined unjustifiably. If they have done something wrong, they do not mind being punished. If they have been trying to accomplish something and have not been able to—because either they don't understand or they have a physical difficulty—their punishment in such circumstances can easily destroy any trust the horse may have in you and damage your relationship. Some horses, particularly geldings, will apparently cope with unreasoned discipline well, but even so it must confuse them.

There are times when you are sure he is misbehaving—a naughty toss of the head, perhaps a buck, whatever; you know your own horse and can tell when he is definitely being naughty. In this case a smack is appropriate. But then if you are not sure . . . you wonder whether to scold him or whether to force him to repeat the movement. You wonder if your explanation has not been clear to the horse and if you should try again. There is a simple answer. Presume the latter: presume you got it wrong, not the horse, and explain it more carefully this time. Unless you are absolutely sure he is being disobedient you must presume confusion or physical difficulty. Otherwise you risk a fight with your horse, which you may not win. Whatever the cause, he will be left with unpleasant memories and perhaps unfortunate associations with the movement forever. You may feel that failure to punish him for a disobedience is letting him get away with it. In fact, because you are asking him to repeat the movement, this is not so. He will think that his bad behavior wasn't worth the effort, because it made no difference. Despite his protest you are still making him do what he didn't want to.

When you reexplain it to him, imagine at the same time that he finds it physically difficult to do. Your task now is to go through the back door to his senses, his intelligence and his physical ability. Don't meet him head on ready for an argument and a fight. Ask him to do something easy that is perhaps similar to what

CHAPTER 7

THE TEMPERAMENT OF HORSES

HORSES ARE ALL DIFFERENT

Horses come in a variety of mentalities. They are just as diverse as human beings. Some are cowardly, some nervous, some tense and some dominant. Others are gentle, high-spirited, brave or lazy. Some are affectionate, some brutish, some sensible and calm, while others are skittish or stupid. There is no such thing as an average horse. They are not machines built to an exact physical and mental design. They all have their quirks, their weaknesses, their hang-ups and their strengths. Therefore, if we are to school horses intelligently, we need to understand not only the physiology and psychology of horses in general, but also the individual physique and mentality of each horse we school. We must use our intelligence to work out a way of schooling that suits them as individuals.

HORSES CHANGE

Never stop reevaluating your horse. As you school him, his mind and body develop and change. Mentally and physically, he becomes a different being. As he changes you must be aware of the metamorphosis and constantly rethink your schooling methods. What worked two months ago may not work today! Remember also that horses' moods can change a lot with the seasons—in the case of mares, with their cycles; and for all horses, in relation to the weather and their food. They also develop and change as they age and mature. Horses also alter in character and sometimes in temperament as their training progresses. Hence this examination of their character is not a static thing. It needs to be constantly reassessed.

MALES VERSUS FEMALES

There are general and well-known differences between mares, geldings and stallions. There is an expression: you tell a gelding, ask a mare and discuss it with a stallion. Needless to say, this is a generalization; but by and large geldings are more laid back and will cope with being pushed around, and even with a bit of unfair treatment. They are relatively easy to deal with. Mares, however, are more sensitive and will resent a rough or unthinking rider. A lot of people won't have mares for this reason. But the truth is, if you are unable to handle a mare, you really aren't such a good rider. They require tact and caring riding, which some people—most particularly impatient men—cannot cope with. If a mare is unjustifiably punished she will be very upset and let her rider know it. If a mare is rewarded for good work she will repay you twice over in her efforts to please you. Being female myself I can quite empathize and sympathize with this behavior. There is another saying, that a bad mare is the worst horse, but a good mare is the best. I am sure this is also true, so long as their riders are capable of bringing out the best in them.

THE CHARACTERS OF YOUR HORSE

A trainer must recognize what type his horse is, so that he knows how to deal with him and get the best out of him. Each horse has a basic temperament type, which is often easy to spot. But he will also have other quirks, likes and dislikes that may take a little time to work out. Take some time to study him, his reactions and his manners. Examine his personality and behavior under a microscope, so that you know how he, as an individual, will take to the training you give him. If you know him well you can adapt your training to suit him and also be ready for what may happen. Preparation will help you to deal with potentially difficult situations.

Horses can be slow-witted or intelligent, lazy or energetic, tense or calm, affectionate or unaffectionate and nasty, well-mannered or ill-mannered, confident or sensitive. These basic temperaments are the core of the horse's personality and rarely change during his life. We can mold their behavior through training, but underneath they are still the same personality. A nasty horse can be taught manners and a lazy horse can be made to perform with more energy, but all the time we are fighting against nature: the job of molding them is hard and their basic personality will often rise to the surface.

Slow learners: Some horses aren't very intelligent. Where another horse might understand a lesson immediately, this one won't. If you know your horse is dull-witted and slow learning, you will need more patience when you teach him a new lesson. You must think of other ways of getting him to do as you wish, ways that won't stress his brain too much. You are his teacher. Like all good teachers, you must find the best way of communicating your information to your pupil.

Quick learners: If he learns lessons quickly and is easily bored, keep his brain occupied and stretched. Be careful not to put strain on his body by making the lessons too advanced if he is mentally further ahead than he is physically.

Nervous horses: If you know your horse is nervous, you will realize that there is no mileage in getting cross with him: you will make him crazy. Instead you must teach him calmly and avoid doing anything that might set off his tension. Read in the chapter on tension (see chapter 8) the ways in which you can help him to be more relaxed.

Lazy horses: It is very frustrating to ride a horse that plods slowly wherever it goes. They will only trot after a lot of effort from the rider's legs, and then it is often a slow trot. Canter is another thing altogether—almost impossible! Increasing the level of concentrated feed and cutting down on the amount of hay or grass may make these animals more energetic. An energetic rider may also help by constantly demanding more from him and never accepting his natural slowness.

Energetic horses: They love to move fast and, as long as they aren't tense, are a joy to ride. Some of these horses can become impatient when you ask them to work more slowly, particularly in situations where there are other horses passing them. If their speed and enthusiasm is a problem, it may help if you reduce their concentrated feed. It may also be worthwhile considering using a stronger bit.

Affectionate, unaffectionate or nasty horses: Horses are often born either affectionate or unaffectionate but their treatment by humans can make a difference. If a horse has been deprived of affection, he will become withdrawn and unable to give it. This situation can be reversed when a human gives time, love and attention to his horse. It is also important that the horse holds his handler in respect. You would rarely engender love and affection from a horse that is undisciplined. Inevitably there are horses that are unaffectionate or nasty by nature and no amount of love, attention and/or discipline would induce them to return it.

Well-mannered and ill-mannered horses: You may well think that the manners of the horse lie in the discipline and training that he is given. For the most part you would be right, but some horses are born with good manners. They never barge past you or stand on your toes or drag you out of the stable. They stop when you stop and carefully walk around you if you are in the way. Then there are the horses who never seem to know or care where their feet are. If they want to go

somewhere, they just go; if someone is in the way, they just blast through them or over them and never around them. Yes, they can be improved through training, but there will still be an occasion when they forget and trample you or drag you in their enthusiasm to get where they are going.

Confident horses: There are some horses that feel good about themselves and about life. They don't worry a great deal, little seems to frighten them and they are happy taking on new situations and challenges.

Sensitive horses: Some horses can be phased by the big occasions like a large show. This sensitivity is normally manifested by nervousness but some horses become quiet and withdrawn and are not able to give their best. The more they experience these occasions, the less it affects them and the quicker they will feel at ease. Be aware that some horses do not show tension but bottle it up inside them. On the surface they appear to be calm, sensible creatures—but underneath this calm exterior, all is turmoil. If your horse might fit into this category, give him as much time and consideration as you would give an outwardly tense horse.

Some horses are sensitive to being pressured in their work. Even though they may be physically capable of doing the work, they cannot cope with the mental strain. Others get upset if they are shouted at or smacked unjustifiably. They may show this sensitivity by becoming tense or by being withdrawn. It is often difficult to tell how much work horses can cope with, so it is always wise to "make haste slowly" with them.

Many horses are upset when they move home. It takes them a while to settle into the new and strange environment. Meanwhile they can be quiet and unhappy. Such horses need to be treated particularly kindly and sympathetically during this time. Extra attention will help them settle in. They need to make friends, both equine and human, so offer your friendship and bond with them. Such horses settle better when they know the routine of their new home, and also know where they fit into the hierarchy of their human and equine companions. It is also a time to take advantage of their insecurity, by showing them the standards of behavior you require, right at the beginning. It is much easier to become

the boss at this time. Just as a new member in a club is given the rules when he joins, so must you give your horse a list of rules when he enters the new environment. It is relatively easy to establish behavior at first, but it becomes increasingly difficult to later change what has become established.

MATCH HORSE TO RIDER

The temperament of the rider should complement the temperament of the horse. If you are a timid rider, you should not ride a dominant or a high-spirited horse. He would either dominate you or frighten you to death. If you are a laid-back rider, you should not ride a lazy horse. You will get nowhere slowly. Conversely, if you have a fiery or energetic temperament, you would not be well matched on a fiery or energetic horse. The two of you would go everywhere at a hundred miles an hour!

I remember a pony, a beautiful chestnut mare, bought for our daughter who was then about 11 years old. It was a high-spirited and nervous animal and my daughter was intent on success. She was motivated and forward thinking. She was constantly being run away with by the pony

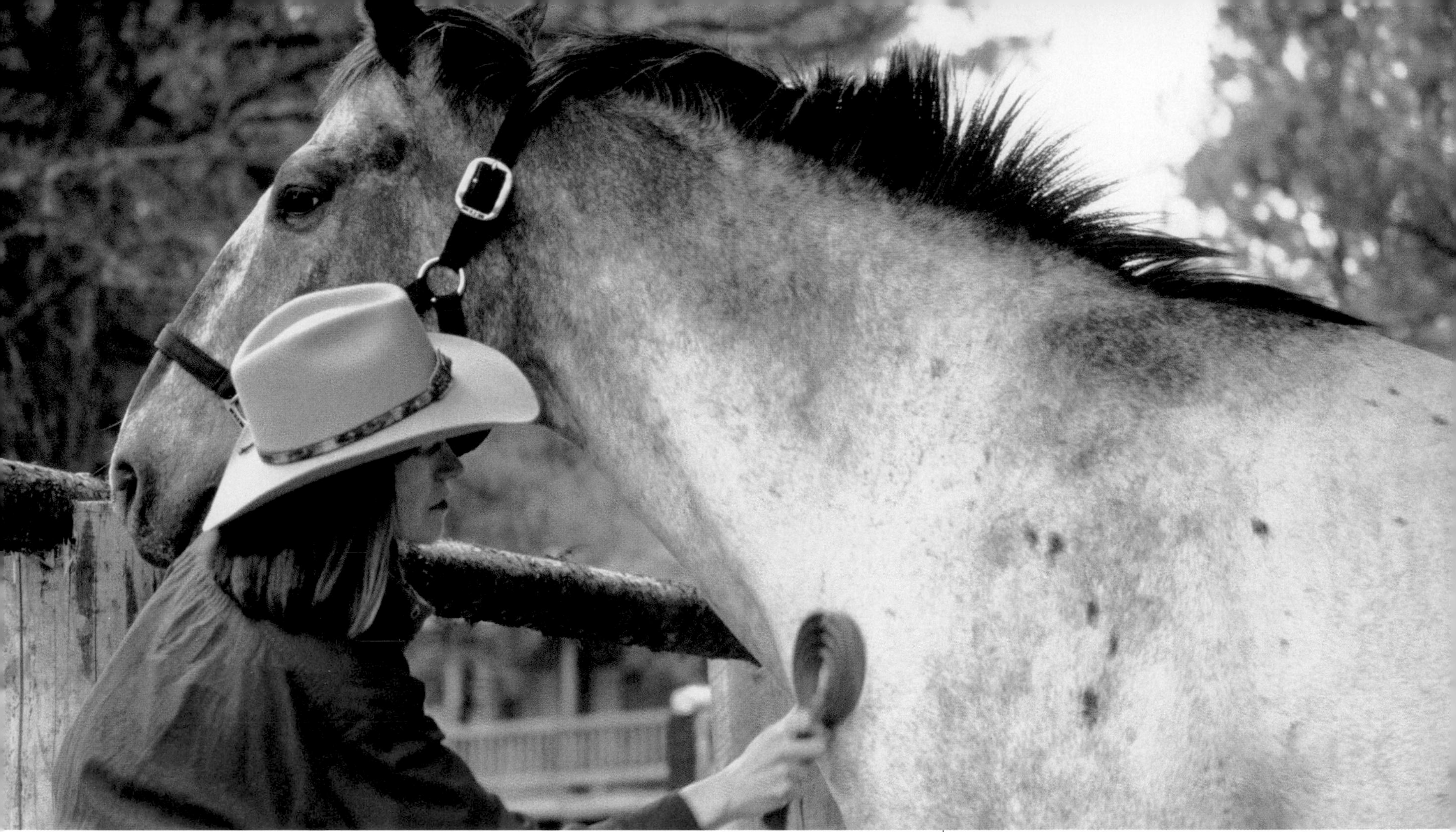

and in the end we had to decide to sell her. We thought finding a suitable home for her would be impossible, and that she would need a strong, competent rider. We were astounded when a small, gentle child came to try her and instantly transformed the pony into a gentle, calm creature. The two became a strong and loving partnership. The pony just needed love and gentle handling, which our daughter at that stage of her life wasn't able to give her.

TEACHING METHODS TO SUIT THE HORSE

Your teaching regime should match the pupil. If he is easily bored, keep him interested with varied lessons. If he learns lessons really quickly, teach him more. If he finds concentrating for a long time hard, keep the lessons short. If he is excitable, make the lessons boring so that he will settle. If he is a stubborn animal who refuses to do something, and you wish to avoid a stand-up battle, find a way to trick him into doing it without his realizing. You could also try this approach if he is willful and disobedient. But if it doesn't work, you will need to stand up to him fearlessly and make him know he has to do as you wish.

The list of different temperaments is almost inexhaustible. You must use your own brain to work out who your horse is and how you should handle him best.

A HAPPY HORSE

Your horse's state of mind is crucial. A happy horse who cares for his rider, and feels his rider cares for him, will perform much better than the horse who is made to perform grudgingly. Strive to build up a trusting relationship with one another by treating him fairly and by not overstraining him. Make your time together fun. He should always be your friend, and he should know it. He should want to do what you want. What a horse learns to do happily he enjoys more, and therefore gives more effort and performs better. When you are schooling, reward and rest frequently. If there is strain, discomfort or shouting—or anything else unpleasant—the horse associates this with what you are asking him to do and may never do it happily or to his best. Unpleasant memories remain with him for a long time and will spoil the work he associates them with. Try to inject pleasure into what you are doing. Whenever you can, steer away from discomfort, strain or pain. Avoid punishment unless it is absolutely necessary.

Imagine a child having piano lessons who was shouted at, criticized and whose knuckles were rapped. Compare this to a child who was praised often, rarely scolded, and whose teacher made the lessons fun. Even if the first child is motivated to be a pianist, that desire is soon knocked out of him. He makes no extra efforts for the tutor. His playing lacks inspiration and joy. It has been forced out of the child. You know it when you hear him playing. The child taught kindly, however, takes pleasure in learning new lessons and seeks to please the tutor. This child's playing reflects the joy he finds in the music.

So is it with horses. A bullied horse performs grudgingly. He lacks the inspiring and energetic movement that should reflect the joy he has found in performing well and pleasing his rider. You have more chance of finding this in a horse ridden by a caring, thinking rider. He makes the lessons less arduous and more pleasant by praising and rewarding the horse—and by not being overly demanding.

The confidence and respect that we hope to achieve from our horse does not come easily. It has to be worked for. Your brain has to work overtime on ways to keep him working happily. But it is not just as easy as that. You also have to earn his respect and his obedience. Combining these two is not so straightforward.

This relationship will be stretched to its limit at times when you have to push your horse to work harder than he feels he wants to. Above all, he is an athlete, and the training of an athlete is demanding. You have to remember that, without pain, there is often no gain, and balance it with the knowledge of just how far you can take it. Try and make every schooling session fun. Avoid over-tiring, over-stressing, overstraining or boring your horse. Particularly avoid getting cross or losing your temper with him. Keep your training interesting and varied, and praise and rest your horse frequently. Your horse should look forward to the next schooling session: he should never dread it. If the work you are doing is particularly hard or stressful, don't make the lesson last for too long. A tiny achievement can sometimes be enough. Just occasionally a lesson may need to be long if he is struggling to understand what you want. Perhaps you could explain it better to him, or maybe there is no other way but to slog on. If this does happen, make it the exception, otherwise your lessons will be anticipated as periods of torture.

It is possible to achieve quite a lot in a short time, either because the horse is naturally talented and athletic, or by demanding a lot of him. A horse has to work at his own pace, which is determined by his natural mental and physical ability. If you can understand your horse and what he is trying to tell you, it should be apparent how much work he can cope

with. If he is pushed too hard, he has no joy in his work because he associates it with discomfort. When you are working your horse, be aware of how he is feeling. Always listen to what he is trying to say to you.

NO PAIN NO GAIN

There is, needless to say, a flip side to this sympathetic, gentle way of training. Developing your horse's athletic ability is something he does not find easy. The degree of difficulty depends partly on his own natural ability and partly on the level to which you wish to take him. It is comparable to a body builder trying to improve his physique in a gym, or perhaps the gruelling training of a ballet dancer. It may involve many, many hours of hard, repetitive work. If you wish to do this work in the gym or become a ballet dancer, the motivation is already there. It is your decision. But it was not your horse's decision to take on this degree of work. He is not always as keen as you might be to achieve the end goal, nor on the work that will take him there. Inevitably, then, there are times when he finds the work hard and resents it, and so there must be times when you will have to push

him where he doesn't want to go. It is then that you have to use all your skill and tact to persuade him to carry on. It may be hard for him but, unless you are prepared to make him, and unless he is prepared to do it, he will not progress beyond his current level. It is at times like these, and there may be many of them, that your domination has to be asserted and followed through. He has to know you are the boss.

When muscles have to be worked hard to develop strength, and when the body has to be stretched, it is hard for him—and you have to insist. So much slogging has to take place to improve the performance: it is often tough and very tedious, with great gaps when nothing seems to be achieved at all. If your horse has developed trust in you, he is more inclined to do as you ask when you have to ask him to work hard. He knows you do not drive him unmercifully on when he is aching, tired and uncomfortable. When you hit one of these schooling sessions, whisper to your horse "no pain no gain." If he trusts you, and if he is listening to you, your relationship will hopefully continue unscathed. What you achieve is a horse that feels himself so much your partner that he wants what you want. Your joy becomes his joy, your achievement his achievement!

CHAPTER 8

Tension

Tension is part of the temperament of horses. But it is such a big topic, it deserves a chapter of its own.

A TENSE MIND

A tense horse can never produce his best work. This particularly applies to dressage and showing, but it is also important in other equestrian spheres. He is too wound up with his tension to concentrate properly on what he is doing, or on what you are asking him to do. At the least, it can be distracting. At the worst, it can totally ruin his performance, send him haywire and possibly make him dangerous. To do his job properly he must be relaxed. It is just as important to have a relaxed horse when you are training him as when you are at competitions. Perhaps you need a calm horse even more when you are riding out on the roads. If your horse is constantly spooking at real or imaginary things in the hedge or elsewhere, it makes your ride both unpleasant and dangerous. When he leaps out away from what frightens him, he may well leap into the path of a passing car.

A TENSE BODY

If a horse is tense in his mind, he is also tense in his body. A tense body cannot use itself properly because it is not relaxed. The horse must be relaxed if he is to be athletic. The tension makes his body stiff, and hence it lacks the flexibility it needs in order to work properly. Each muscle and ligament is tight and constricted. The back is rigid, inflexible and possibly hunched. Each step is short and staccato. Tension totally mars the physical performance of any horse. A tense body can never perform well, or anywhere near its maximum.

DIFFERENT TYPES OF TENSION

Most horses, when stressed, become jumpy and tense. Some manifest their tension by becoming faster in their work, rushing everything they do. Some become irritable and their character changes. They flatten their ears and threaten to bite when, otherwise, they would be sweet natured. Occasionally

horses who are stressed "go into themselves"— becoming unusually quiet and unmotivated. These horses often hang well back in company and go much more slowly than usual.

Causes of Tension

THE NATURE OF THE HORSE

Some horses are tense by nature. It is difficult, or impossible, to change these horses and make them any less tense. However, you can capitalize on certain equine tendencies. For example, most horses are calmer in an environment in which they feel safe, and less calm in unfamiliar places. By frequently exposing them to the unfamiliar environment, they may grow to regard it as a familiar one and relax.

A show ground may be something new for your horse. When he is there, he may be tense and therefore underperform. You could keep away from all shows because of this. A tense horse at a show is both frightening and depressing. But, if you want him to get used to shows, make a particular point of going to as many as you can. Make the gap between shows as short as possible. After six or so shows you should find that your horse begins to regard them as familiar, and he becomes less tense. If you didn't compete in the first few shows, this would be a further reason for the horse to relax. Try to remember, while there, to be calm yourself. A horse's tension easily passes onto the rider, and then back to the horse. It becomes a vicious circle of tension which only you can break.

HORSES WHO HAVE BEEN MADE TENSE

Pain, fear, and fear of pain are all very potent, and understandable, causes of tension. If a horse has been frightened or hurt, then he will be tense when confronted with the cause of the fear or hurt again. He could be remembering an accident, or perhaps he has been overfaced at a jump. Because of their incredible memories, it is difficult to make horses understand that the same things will not happen again. You have to teach your horse that these situations are no longer dangerous. You achieve this by repeatedly exposing him to similar circumstances and being sure that nothing horrible happens. The horse comes to realize that his fears are no longer justified. For example, if a horse has been overfaced, by jumping too high, he may have become frightened of all jumps. If he can now be persuaded to jump over tiny obstacles, he begins to realize that there are some jumps he can manage. It is better to jump several small jumps, six or seven times over a week or two. Let it really sink in that he can manage to do it and that nothing awful is going to happen to him when he does. Only jump a few jumps each time. Make a big fuss after he has jumped. Teach him to associate jumping with pleasure. Hopefully the memory of the pain or fear will go away. Later on, you can gradually increase the height of the jumps, taking care to avoid overfacing him again.

Large jumps, or the possibility of pain, are not the only things that can frighten horses. Difficult or strenuous flat work can be too demanding and can cause them to fear all work on the flat. If the horse is otherwise calm until you start to school him on the flat, presume that something too strenuous has been asked of him. Try asking the horse to perform only very easy tasks for a week or two, keeping the lessons short and fun and rewarding the horse afterwards. This should help cure his fear of flat work.

If you can remember what work you had done before the tension occurred, and what had actually caused the tension, you can prevent its recurrence. It is probable that the horse wasn't strong enough, or supple enough, to cope with the level of work required. If taking his work to a new pitch makes him tense, presume the harder work is the reason for the tension. Resume the easier work, and concentrate on exercises that will make him strong enough for the next level. You need to make sure he is always fully ready for the next level of work before you ask for it. Never teach something new or difficult when the horse is tired.

BAD BEHAVIOR

Sometimes a horse may behave badly and you know that the reason is tension. Something may have frightened him, or he may be tense for another reason. You may feel that it really isn't worth working your horse when he is like this. Perhaps you have been there before, and no matter how long you worked him, he wouldn't behave. Scolding him certainly never made him behave better.

On occasions like this the very worst thing you could do is stop working him. This effectively rewards him for wrong behavior. It is essential that you carry on work until he is well behaved again, even if only for a short while. You must always finish on a good note because that is where you will start the next time. Stretch your imagination to find ways of making him behave. Ask him for very easy work. Change the place where you work if there is somewhere else that he feels more secure. Stroke him and talk to him to calm him down. Try singing to him: this may calm him, or maybe not! Perhaps if you worked him in walk on a long rein for a while he might be better. There are so many reasons why a horse could be badly behaved and so many potential cures, it is impossible to mention them all here. You must get to know your horse and learn what should help him.

Only when he has given you some good work should you finish the lesson. It doesn't matter what tactics you use to produce the good work, as long as you get it. As long as you win.

Riding a horse unsympathetically or even cruelly—shouting at him or beating him repeatedly—is cause for the horse to worry about whether this is going to happen again, and the consequence is tension.

Horses can appear to be two personalities at once. They can be both tense, and

at the same time disobedient or naughty. The one seems to grow out of the other. Like many humans, because they are frightened or tense, they become confused and sometimes aggressive. When the horse becomes badly behaved, it is easy to overlook the fact that fear made him like this in the first place, and it is easy to scold him for his naughtiness. Unfortunately this increases his fear and makes the behavior worse. This is why it is so important to try to keep the horse happy, not by giving in to him, but by understanding him. You must ask him to do what you want in a way that he will understand and find easy—mentally and physically.

It is important to recognize the horse who is naughty because of fear as distinct from the horse who is naughty just because he is naughty. If the fearful horse misbehaves, keep cool. Calm him down. Then, quietly and firmly, explain to him again what you want him to do and ask him to do it again. If what you have asked may be a little hard for him, ask him to do something similar, but easier.

If your horse or his behavior frightens you, or makes you tense or angry, it shows in the way you han-

dle him. You must overcome these emotions before you continue working, because they make you rough or unsure in your actions and your horse will react badly. If you are rough, it will frighten him or make him tense. This will make him behave badly. If you are nervous, he knows it. He can tell that you are not a confident, strong person able to look after him and tell him what to do. This confuses him, makes him feel insecure, and his behavior becomes even worse. Always ride calmly and confidently. You pass these feelings onto your horse and make him calm and confident too. If you are frightened or angry, and you reveal these emotions, you make him fearful. You must be a good actor and become a calm, confident person. The Method school of acting is preferred. You should try and turn yourself into a calm person, rather than pretending to be one.

TENSE RIDERS

If a rider is tense the horse knows. The rider's legs grip the horse's sides and so he feels the tension of the rider through the legs as they grip. He thinks the rider wants him to go forwards more. So off he goes. This probably makes the rider feel even more nervous and grab the reins, which in turn will make the horse even more tense. Also, a tense rider does not flex his back. As he comes down onto the saddle he doesn't absorb his own body weight properly. He comes down heavily on the horse's spine. This also upsets the horse, possibly hurts him and, quite understandably, makes him tense.

A horse ridden like this cannot be happy. He is uncomfortable because of the gripping, the tight reins and/or the rigid back of the rider. The tension of the rider comes through to the horse immediately, because horses are so well attuned to the feel of our bodies. The horse wonders what there is to be tense about, and he too becomes tense. Unless the rider can relax and ride in a relaxed manner, the horse cannot be relaxed. Hence a tense rider causes a horse to become tense. If a horse is ridden by a tense rider for a long time, he may become permanently tense. He may take on the personality of his trainer.

A tense rider does not make decisions well and is afraid of the horse. This fear may show in aggression or

201

impatience. Try to recognize fear in yourself, and avoid the temptation to react against the horse. It could well be that you are both frightened of each other! It is not unusual to see a nervous person hit out at a horse who has frightened him. Quite often the cause of the incident is a tense horse, reacting nervously by shying, or lifting his head, or stepping sideways, or some other misdemeanor. This frightens the nervous rider or handler who hits the horse in retaliation, feeling the horse has been naughty. Inevitably this leads the horse to be even more nervous and tense. If the rider only had the sense to realize that the horse was tense in the first place, he would stroke and soothe the horse rather than making the tension worse by hitting him. You can probably recognize occasions when you have been a little unsure of, or intimidated by, a horse. You became tense and unable to ride and treat the horse as well as you ought. If a horse makes you nervous, it is indeed difficult to remain calm and handle him confidently. But, if you are anything less than calm, you will make him even more frightened and even more frightening. It is back to acting—and pretending to be calm even when you are not.

WIND

Horses, particularly those with a tendency toward nervousness, frequently become tense when it is windy. Their hearing is impaired by the noise of the wind. Sounds, which would normally be audible to them, are carried away on the wind, or drowned out by the noise of the wind. A horse's hearing is normally very acute. He uses this facility in the wild, and in domesticated life, to keep him safe. If a potential threat were obscured from sight the horse would hear it. Knowing he is so well able to hear makes him more relaxed. Deprived of his ability to hear by the wind, he becomes overalert, reacting to everything that moves. He tries to substitute sight for hearing and will twitch this way and that to see all around him. Naturally, he is nervous and tense because he has less warning of a predator's approach. He is constantly on the alert and ready to flee. This tension is a self-protection mechanism.

Frequent exposure (see page 18) is unlikely to work with wind. To be nervous when he cannot hear is so much a part of a horse's nature that no amount of exposure to wind will convince him that he is safe.

A horse who is well disciplined and trusts his rider is better behaved in the wind than other horses. Even so, his level of concentration is often affected by the attention he diverts in trying to hear over the noise of the wind, and see what he cannot hear.

INCORRECT OR OVERFEEDING (PARTICULARLY RICH GRASS IN SPRING)

If the horse's digestive system is overloaded with rich spring grass (or sometimes early autumn grass), or too much hard feed, it produces toxins that will make him crazy. The differing metabolism of horses makes this problem less in some horses than in others. Fine bodied, thoroughbred types tend to suffer less than heavier built horses whose metabolism is slower.

If your horse is affected by rich grass, reduce its availability or put him on poorer pasture. Or consider using a magnesium supplement (see page 118).

It is easy to overdo the amount of hard feed. This will also cause horses to be excitable. Our natural desire to do the best for our horses often leads us to overfeed them, rather like an indulgent mother feeding her increasingly obese children. If your horse has been made crazy by too much feed, reduce it to an absolute minimum, perhaps only feeding hay. Keep it there for several days. If too much feed is causing the problem, you should begin to notice a difference—and sanity should start returning. If, on this lower level of feed, the horse maintains his physical condition and has enough energy for the work he is doing, keep to it. However, if he loses condition, or doesn't have sufficient energy, increase the hard feed by a small amount. Every two or three days, gradually step up the feed level, until you reach the point where it supplies him with sufficient energy for the

work you wish him to do, but without returning to silly behavior. The diet you choose must suit your horse as an individual. There is no guide that can be given as to amounts of feed, because each horse's requirements are so different.

STRANGE SURROUNDINGS OR CIRCUMSTANCES

A horse who has never been to a competition or any gathering of horses before will naturally be nervous of all the activity—and the presence of so many horses doing strange things. This tends to pass after the horse has been to several such occasions in close succession (frequent exposure). Some horses panic when seeing sheep, or donkeys (particularly braying ones), at close quarters for the first time. Most horses are thrown into a complete fit when they see pigs. If they see them frequently, they may become less upset by them, although the fear of pigs is often maintained even then.

RIDER'S LACK OF DISCIPLINE

Either the rider or the horse must be the dominant partner in the relationship. If the rider does not assert his domination, then it follows that the horse is the dominant one. In this case, the horse only does as the rider wants when it suits him. He believes that he is in control of the situation (as he is) and therefore is responsible for what happens. Because of this, he, instead of the rider, has to make the decisions. This often causes the horse to be nervous and insecure.

This is a little bit like an adult and a child going into a potentially dangerous situation together—for example, crossing the road. If the adult is in charge, the child feels relaxed, relying on the competence and knowledge of the older person. Normally the adult holds the child's hand securely and totally takes over. The child relaxes because he trusts the adult, who, carefully and calmly, takes them both safely across the road. If the child were crossing the road on his own, he would be agitated and tense, looking from side to side and studying the road. When he judged it safe, he would probably run across to the other side. He would not enjoy the experience. His heart may be pounding afterwards. In the same way, if the horse felt dominated by the rider, he would relax. This is because he knows the rider is strong, will make the right decisions, and will look after him. He does not worry about what to do next. The rider will tell him. If he thinks the rider won't tell him, if he has to make all the decisions himself, he will be tense.

DISCIPLINE

Sometimes horses misbehave and you have to discipline them, either by smacking or by raising your voice. Some horses, particularly those of a

sensitive nature, get upset if they are disciplined, even if they deserve it. Some of them then behave worse than before! You may often presume that this bad behavior is further naughtiness, so naturally you scold him again. This makes his behavior worse still. But in fact, this second misdemeanor is caused by tension because he is upset at being scolded. After the first discipline, which perhaps cannot be avoided, immediately make up with your horse. Remind him that you still love him with a stroke and a gentle word. If he is this sensitive type of horse, he requires very little in the way of discipline. A verbal reprimand will often be sufficient.

RIDER'S INCONSISTENCY

The rider needs to make it absolutely clear what he wants. If he is unclear in the aids, or incapable of insisting that the horse is obedient to the aids, this can result in a confused horse. He does not know what the rider wants, and therefore has to make some of the decisions himself. It is much easier for a horse if the rider is in control. The horse can then relax. A consistent rider tends to produce a calmer horse. Your horse must always know what you want him to do.

UNNATURAL LIFESTYLE

A horse cooped up for days, weeks, months or even years on end in a stable, only being allowed out for work, is much more likely to suffer from tension than a horse allowed to graze most days.

ANTICIPATION

A horse may become tense because he is expecting something to happen that he very much likes, or very much dislikes. For example, suppose you are teaching your horse a new maneuver, one with which he has physical or mental difficulty. Asking him to perform it may make him tense—and this is understandable. But he may also be tense because he thinks you are going to ask him to perform it, even if you haven't mentioned it to him. Perhaps you have worked on it every day at about the same time and it is approaching that time now. He may be expecting it and this expectation makes him tense. Perhaps you have already asked him for it and are now moving onto something different, but he is still expecting it.

Anticipating something good can also make a horse tense. The other day I rode my horse at a different time than usual. It was in the late afternoon, before she had had her feed. My normally quiet animal was doing everything at such a rate of knots. She thought her feed would be in the stable when she returned, and she couldn't wait to get to it. Strangely, I experienced a similar sensation shortly afterwards when I was preparing my own food. I was hungry and it looked so tempting, I found myself rushing the preparation. The anticipation of the food had definitely made me tense. Horses are nearly always tense just before feed arrives, or before they go outside. A gelding I have always stales just before he has his feed and just before he goes outside—a strange way of showing tension but not uncommon! Some horses are tense just before you ride them and misbehave when you are tacking them up. Whether this is because they are anticipating a good experience or a bad one I am not sure!

Cures for Tension

Tension increases the speed at which the heart beats. We can try to lower the heart rate and relax the horse by stroking him on his withers, just as an equine grooming friend might do. This is particularly useful when you are riding, as your hands are right by his withers. Talking to him in a soothing voice can also induce relaxation. Sometimes the horse can be too tense to take any notice of what you are doing. Don't give up too soon, because it can sometimes take a while to cut into the tension and get through to him.

If your horse is a tense type, try to find situations in which he is less tense. Use these for training, perhaps after he has been out at grass for an hour or two. A horse who has been out grazing will often be more relaxed than a horse who has been stabled for hours or days. If there is much grass on the field, beware of damaging the lungs. The stomach lies near to the lungs. When the horse works, his lungs need to expand to provide more oxygen for his working body. If the stomach is full, there is less room for the lungs to expand, putting strain on the existing lung capacity and possibly causing damage.

If you need to take advantage of a full stomach to gain a quiet horse, keep the work undemanding, and never let the horse's breathing become at all fast. The most practical way is to ride your horse perhaps half an hour after he has been fed a smallish feed of concentrates, at a time when the stomach is no longer full but the horse doesn't yet feel hungry again. Think of the rather contented feeling you have after a meal. You are much less likely to be edgy and tense then. But because your stomach is full, you don't feel too much like running around either. Half an hour later would be better.

If your horse spends too much time in the stable with nothing to do, put him out in a field more often or for longer. If he lacks company, particularly equine, give him some. If his way of life is close to nature he has more chance of having a relaxed personality.

It is up to you as a thinking rider to work out why your horse is tense and, if possible, try to devise methods of making him less tense.

USE OF TRANQUILIZERS

These do have the desired effect of making the horse less tense but, unfortunately, make the horse drowsy and unable to perform safely.

MAGNESIUM DEPLETION

When the horse is suffering from magnesium depletion he can become very tense. A horse suffering from hypomagnesemia can also be irritable, unwilling and generally not his usual self. This tension can last for a long time—until he has sufficient magnesium in his system again. Stress can cause the horse to lose more magnesium from his system than normal. Circumstances such as a change of routine, cold weather, an accident, his first few competitions, traveling (particularly on a long journey), very hard work or any kind of a stressful or frightening situation can cause such a loss. Unfortunately, modern farming methods tend not to provide sufficient levels of magnesium to allow this depletion to be restored naturally.

Magnesium deficiency can also be caused by rich grass, or overfeeding of concentrates.

There are several products on the market containing magnesium. They can have a magic effect on the temperament of a horse suffering a deficiency. Within a matter of days he should be back to his normal self. I personally have used a product by Triple Crown called NOMAD that contains partly chelated, and therefore easily absorbed, magnesium. If you have a horse who gets tense in certain situations, such as a show, consider feeding him a supplement of magnesium for a few days beforehand.

HERBAL AND HOMEOPATHIC REMEDIES

Some people swear by them, others find them useless. The answer must be to try them and see how they suit your horse.

There is another product manufactured by Triple Crown that deals with tension in horses called Attitude Adjuster. It contains all of the above plus magnesium. Not having any knowledge or experience of the product, I was keen to test it, par-

ticularly before I was prepared to recommend it here! I tried it on a horse of my own and persuaded two other people to try it on their tense animals. In all three horses the results were very impressive. After ten days to two weeks, they were all saner and more relaxed.

One of the horses was problematic all the time, but particularly when being ridden: not staying still when being mounted and spooking at everything on the road. This particular horse also box-walked constantly, leaving his stable in a dreadful mess. After about two weeks on Attitude Adjuster he improved in every way. Even though he was by no means perfect, there was a marked difference and he became much easier to handle and ride. It may be that his bad behavior had become so much a way of life for him that, to some degree, he was still behaving like this out of habit—even though the reason for the behavior, the tension, had gone.

The second horse, a mare, is one who takes her work very seriously and allows it to make her tense. After ten days on Attitude Adjuster she was coping with her work in a much more relaxed manner.

The third horse (my own) was a gelding who I was in the process of backing. When I was lungeing him he would sometimes be naughty. I would scold him, and everything went wrong from that point. He couldn't cope with discipline, yet sometimes he just had to have it. There seemed no way forward until I tried Attitude Adjuster. When he was on it he was much calmer and his behavior improved dramatically. He was rarely naughty and, if he did misbehave, he then coped well with being disciplined. Three out of three seems a pretty good average. I think I could recommend you give it a try.

I have not heard of or experienced any side effects of any of the contents of Attitude Adjuster but cannot vouch for their absence.

I am told by the manufacturers that it is of no use on mares who suffer from cyclical tension, but it is very good on horses who manifest their tension by becoming withdrawn and becoming quiet and slower in performance. I was also told by the manufacturers that, if it was necessary to feed the product long term, it may be possible to reduce the dosage gradually. They suggested sticking with each reduced dosage for approximately a week before cutting it down further. If the symptoms returned during that week, return the dosage to the higher one.

CHAPTER 9

What do Horses enjoy?

Or, more accurately, do horses enjoy anything? And, if so, why? Because we love horses, we like to do things to make them happy: a nice big feed, a warm stable and/or rug, the company of other horses, turning out on a sunny spring day onto a field full of fresh grass. This list is based on what a horse needs for survival: warmth, food and the protection of a group. We enjoy things that we need to survive, so we presume that it is the same for horses. We like the idea that our friends enjoy themselves.

What if we tried adding to this list other things that we enjoy, and feel our horse also enjoys? Galloping with other horses, jumping, hacking out. Are we now in the realms of fantasy? We enjoy them so we refer our enjoyment to the horse. Are we right to make this presumption? They have no need to do these things to survive (except in certain circumstances) but some horses do appear to enjoy themselves at these times. Is it possible to gain some insight into the minds of horses who appear to enjoy some things more than others? Jumping, for example: some horses seem to love it while others exhibit no inclination to jump unless forced.

Why is there this difference? Is it purely liking and disliking, just as some people like apples and others don't, or are there more practical reasons? Do some horses dislike jumping because they are less athletic and therefore have a physical disadvantage? Or is it because they have been trained roughly or badly so that they have a fear of it? Both of these would be understandable reasons.

Some horses appear to enjoy racing. They strive to get to the front of the field. There are others who hang back. They are difficult to persuade to make even the slightest effort to get in front of another horse. You might think that perhaps these animals are naturally slow, but this is not the case. Those same horses who want to be behind are not necessarily slow movers when they are on their own. They just don't like being in front of others. Physical reasons do not explain this. If they can go fast when on their own, then in company they have no physical reason to go slow. We, therefore, have to presume that it is the mentality of the horse that inhibits his performance. He simply doesn't like it. Just as some people like golf and others don't.

What about the flat race trainer who has had horse after horse through his hands and started them all racing? He treated and trained every horse in exactly the same way. They were all bred to race and should have the physical ability. How else could you explain the reason behind their often very differing performances, if not that they either liked or disliked the sport.

We humans need to be constantly on our guard against anthropomorphism with animals. Inevitably, when someone says horses are behaving like humans, the scientific mind immediately wants to reject it. But perhaps, sometimes, we are correct to assume they behave like humans. After all, humans have been able to subdue and ride horses for thousands of years. One reason is the similarities of our two species.

We know that circumstances can cause a horse to dislike certain things. If so, logic suggests it is possible to make a horse like something that he otherwise would

not like. For example, if, every time your horse jumps a jump he is given a pat or a carrot, he learns to associate jumping with nice things. Eventually he may well think he likes jumping, even if he didn't before. This tactic has wider relevance.

Conditioning by pleasure really comes into its own during schooling. If everything that happens during and around the hard or boring work is really pleasant—rests, praise and perhaps treats—the horse thinks of training sessions as

pleasurable. The whole atmosphere of training changes. It should become an uplifting experience for both horse and rider. If you weren't already, you should now be working together as a partnership.

Does the horse have any sense of his owner's enjoyment? If the rider is enthusiastic about, shall we say, hacking out, perhaps the horse picks up some of his owner's happiness and shares it. This is probably an overstatement. More likely the horse enjoys the natural consequences of his rider's joy, such as a pat or an extra feed, and associates that with the hacking out. Even more likely, the horse really does enjoy hacking out, because there is nothing much demanded physically or mentally.

DO HORSES LOVE?

Again we are back to anthropomorphism. We love them so we want them to behave like us and love us back. We would like to think of them as loyal, thinking creatures who, like Champion the Wonder Horse, would come and save us in threatening situations. Although this is definitely stretching reality, there are some horses who do make enormous efforts for their riders, well above and beyond the call of duty.

Horses certainly do display some kind of feeling for humans. Even when there is no feed bowl about, they often watch their owner if they are separated, and nicker happily when they are reunited. There are even some horses who go into decline if separated from their owners for long. So perhaps there is emotion. But would it be fanciful to say that this emotion is love?

First we need to define love. The most obvious kind is based on sexual attraction, which we can discount here. There is also the nonsexual love one could have for a friend. This could be based on shared interests and respect. Then there is the love one has for one's children, which is based on maternal/paternal love and the survival of the species. We are programmed to love our children like this so that we will protect our young. In parallel, there is also the love a child has for its parent. This love is engendered by the need for security and for caring, for strong company. Children are programmed to love the provider of food, warmth, shelter and protection. Such love makes sense if you wish to survive. Now we are getting

nearer to the relationship that horses have for other horses. It is based on survival: finding food, the need of company for protection. If we have supplanted the role of other horses in the life of our horse, then it does not take too great a leap of faith to believe that we have come to occupy the emotional relationship they have for one another. How close it is to the human emotion termed love, we shall never know.

We have seen how horses are givers and receivers of affection when they bond with each other. They display a strong need to belong, and to feel they are cared for. Children give ponies masses of attention and affection. When we grow older, we often presume that, because they are animals, they don't really need this affection. As children we gave it only to satisfy our own desire to give love. But perhaps we are wrong. Perhaps they do like this affection and respond by giving affection in return. If you watch children with their ponies, they certainly do seem to enjoy a very special and rewarding relationship.

During my research for this book I have deliberately increased the amount of care and affection I give to my horses. I have certainly noticed a difference in their attitudes towards me. I enjoy their company more and they are happier because of our changed relationship. As well as being caring to them when I handle them, I am more sympathetic when they are being schooled. I seldom get cross with them. I always take more time to explain things carefully. I don't push them as hard as I used to. I rest them more often if work is stressful. I praise more, and stop work if I feel they have had enough. It all boils down to loving them more and caring about them as individuals. I would never have believed that it could make so much difference to their behavior and their well-being.

The title of this chapter is "What do horses enjoy?" One thing is for certain: they enjoy being loved and treated kindly, and repay doubly the care that they are given.

CHAPTER 10

The Nature of the Rider

The expert rider is armed with many skills and much knowledge. He is a teacher who is able to communicate with his horse and understand his communications and an athlete with the skill and physical ability to ride and school a horse correctly. You are working to produce an animal who has the strength of a body builder with the beauty and grace of a ballet dancer. To create this altered and enhanced animal, you need to understand the mechanics of his motion and balance. You must combine the emotions and skills of a carer and teacher—befriending and loving your horse—with the strengths of a strict master.

Understanding your own nature is important in your ability to train a horse. People are all different, and therefore the relationship you have with your horse differs from the relationship another person would have. It is important to understand your personality and how you relate to your horse. You need to evaluate your strengths and weaknesses so as to build upon the former and improve upon the latter.

It is worth studying the natures and temperaments of successful riders to see if they have anything in common. Is there a temperament that is most suited to the training of horses? Do successful riders have characteristics that we can try and emulate?

Calmness and patience would probably come highest in the list of desirable characteristics and are the most commonly

noticed virtues. A rider who makes an effort to be calm, and think rather than overreact, helps the horse stay calm. It also helps the rider to make the sanest decision if things start to go wrong.

The successful rider has the ability, natural or acquired, to dominate his horse. He instills in the horse the knowledge that the rider is boss and the horse must always do as he is told. He is neither cruel nor does he need violence to obtain obedience or establish domination.

Determination and tenacity are also high on the list. Schooling a horse takes time and there are often setbacks. You must weather the many storms. You cannot give up when things go wrong. A determined rider will try and try again.

A most undesirable characteristic would be impatience or any tendency to short temper. Losing your temper with an animal is always counterproductive.

The ability to bond with the horse and to empathize with his thoughts and feelings is common to most successful trainers. They love and care for their horses almost like their own children. They make sure that everything is right with them. A happy and contented horse who trusts his trainer will give so much more than an unhappy or distrustful horse.

There can't be a successful trainer who isn't also brave. You risk being thrown off when scolding a naughty horse. You are fearless and always assertive in the presence of a potential bullying monster.

You may not have all these characteristics naturally. But, with determination, you can acquire them. Through self-discipline you can become more patient, and with motivation a lot of the rest can be learned.

Tension in riders is a bar to relaxed, sensitive riding. It could be caused by nerves or, perversely, by too much motivation. Overmotivated riders will over ride their horse— push, push, pushing all the time. It wears them out, it wears their horses out, and because there is so much tension, it doesn't even work well. The rider must make a conscious effort to relax. It can help to sing or hum in the rhythm of the horse's gait. The advantages to being a relaxed rider are that the seat is deeper and the reactions calmer. The horse should be calmer too, and the rider should have a better feel of how the horse is going.

A great asset so far unmentioned is talent, the intuitive gift of understanding what to do when and how to do it. It is arbitrarily allocated in different quantities to different people! If you don't possess it, the only alternative is hard work, based on the advice given in books like this one.

CHAPTER 11

Human Balance

Balance is one of the fundamental elements of horsemanship. We need to understand the mechanics behind it. The better balanced we are, the better we will ride and hence be able to teach our horses to balance themselves. We need to understand how the distribution of our weight influences our ability to ride effectively and securely, and how it affects the way in which the horse goes. First we must understand how we balance our own bodies when not riding.

BEING BALANCED

Stand up straight with your weight equally distributed over each leg, your arms down by your sides, and your head in the middle of your shoulders, looking straight ahead. You should now be balanced naturally and able to stand like this fully relaxed, with no tension in any part of your body. Looking at your body from the back or front draw an imaginary vertical line upward from the center of the gap between your feet. See fig. 2a. This line should follow the line of your spine and bisect the center of your head. There should be equal weight on either side of it.

Then, look from the side, as in fig. 2b. Draw an imaginary vertical line upward from a point equal in distance from your heel and the ball of your foot. This line should pass through the middle of your body and head. Here also there should be the same weight on either side of the line.

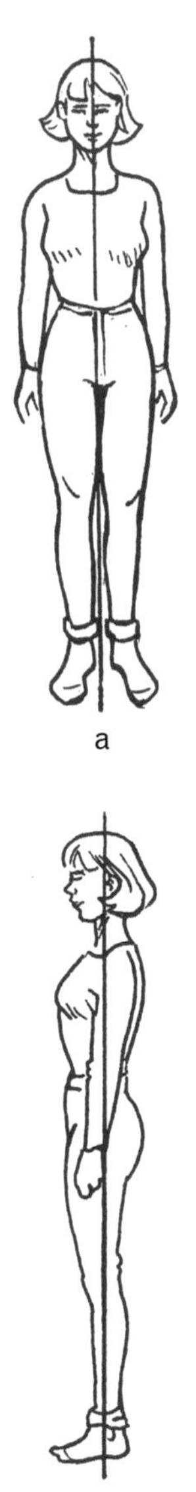

Fig. 2 The human in balance.

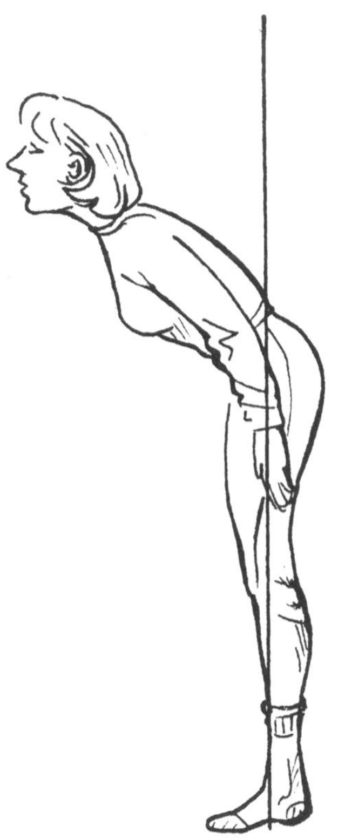

Fig. 3 Out of balance.

IMBALANCED LINEALLY

Tip the upper part of your body forwards slightly, as in fig. 3. Notice the tension and strain this puts on your toes and leg muscles. You have more weight on your toes than on your heels. You are no longer in natural balance. You are straining to avoid falling forwards. If you drew an imaginary vertical line upward from a point equal in distance from your heel and the ball of your foot, there would not be the same amount of weight on either side of the line.

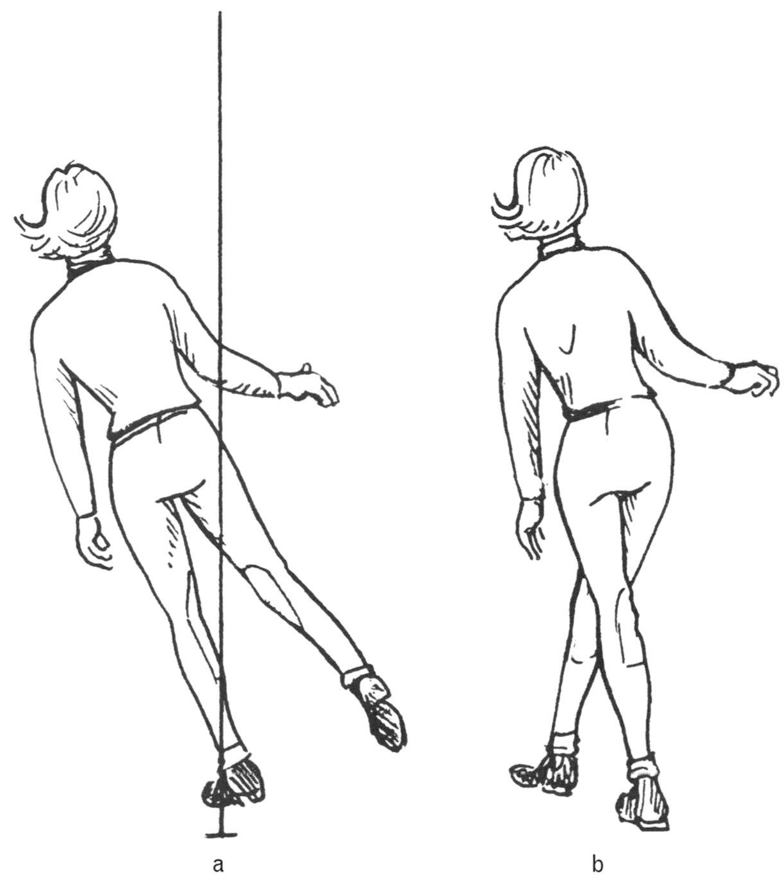

Fig. 4
a = The human out of balance.
b = Correcting the imbalance by stepping under the weight.

IMBALANCED LATERALLY

If you lean sideways you will struggle to balance over one leg. You have more weight on one than on the other. Again, the vertical line drawn up from the middle of the supporting heel would not equally bisect your weight.

For something more exaggerated, lean your whole body to the left, to the extent that you feel you are about to fall over, as shown in fig. 4a. You are now well out of balance. Your body can only compensate for this by taking a step in the di-

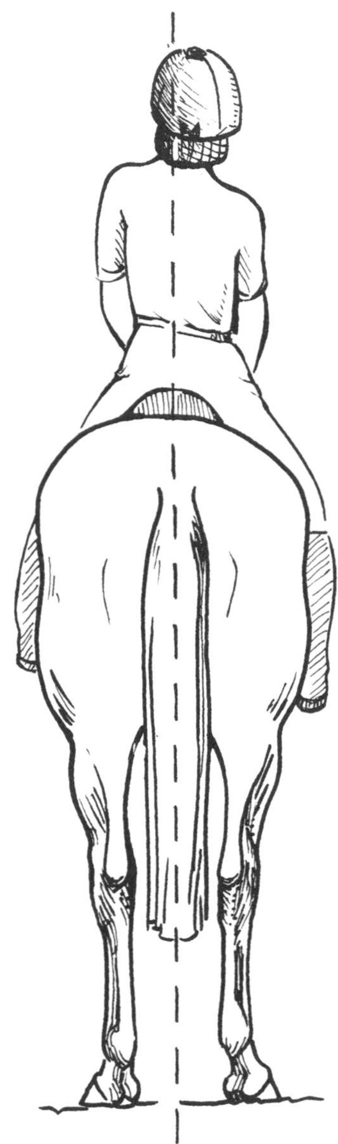

Fig. 5 Too much weight over right hip.

rection in which you are leaning. In effect your legs are coming under you and catching the upper part of your body to prevent you from falling over, as in fig. 4b.

Your body is programmed to keep you upright. It will make adjustments instinctively, that is, without your realizing that you have done anything. Sometimes, if you are out of balance, instead of putting the balance right you tense another part of your body to keep yourself from falling over. Again, you often do not realize that you have done this. This means it is possible to walk (and ride) with more weight on one side of your body than on the other, and be unaware of it! To remain upright when you are out of balance, your body has to tense muscles. This tension possibly affects the whole of your body. Remember how your toes and calves tensed when you leaned forwards slightly. As a nonriding human this imbalance can place strain on your body, eventually causing damage, particularly to the spine. An imbalanced rider can put a disproportionate amount of weight on one side of the horse, causing the horse to be out of balance too. For example, if you ride leaning to one side, as shown in fig. 5, you are putting more weight on the right side of the horse. This lack of balance will make him uncomfortable, tense and desirous of balancing himself by taking a step to the right, just as the person did in fig. 4b.

To be in balance when standing you need equal weight over each leg. When riding, you will be in balance when you have equal weight over each hipbone. Viewed from the back it should be possible to draw a vertical line upward from a point equidistant from each of the horse's back legs. This line should pass up through the tail and spine of the horse then up the spine of the rider and eventually bisect the rider's head. The rider should have equal weight on either side of that line.

The rider in fig. 6, unlike the one in fig. 5, is correctly balanced over the horse's center of gravity and has equal weight over both hip joints.

LATERAL IMBALANCE PRODUCES ADVERSE CONSEQUENCES:

Gripping

If you are not evenly balanced, your legs grip to hold you on, preventing you from having a deep seat, as gripping legs push you to the top of the saddle. The most effective seat is one where the legs are open and relaxed, which allows the rider to sit deeply in the saddle and have the maximum contact with the horse's body.

Gripping creates tension. Tension stops you from being relaxed, which is essential. Tension communicates itself to the horse and makes the horse tense too. A relaxed rider sits deeply in the saddle and feels the movement of the horse. You become part of the movement of the horse, and sense better what is happening beneath you. If you are tense this is impossible.

Gripping confuses the clarity of the leg aids. The legs should only gently touch the sides of the horse. When the leg aids are applied, the legs increase their pressure to give a message to the horse. If, however, the legs are already applying pressure, because you are gripping, then there is no margin for increasing this pressure to tell the horse what you want.

If you ride lopsidedly, you are less secure and therefore unable to ride the horse effectively. Because you are not secure, some of your attention is given to staying on the horse. This applies even if you are only leaning a small amount. You are more concerned about staying on the horse than riding him well. Your legs want to grip in the same position on the horse's sides, rather than move around, as they need to when giving precise aids.

Weight

The horse knows if there is more weight on one side of his body than on the other. He feels that you are about to fall off. His instinctive reaction is to take a step in the direction of the potential fall, to catch your weight.

Imagine carrying a small child on your shoulders. If you've got a small child you can do it for real. When the child leans to one side, as in fig. 7, your immediate reaction is to take a step in the same direction the child is leaning, to step under the weight of the child. The horse will want to do the same thing with you.

We use this displacement of weight as an aid when we want the horse to move sideways. But, if we want to go in a straight line, we must keep our weight absolutely central.

Lineal Balance

Seated on the horse, draw an imaginary line going up vertically from the back of the heel. If a rider is balanced this line should go vertically upwards from the back

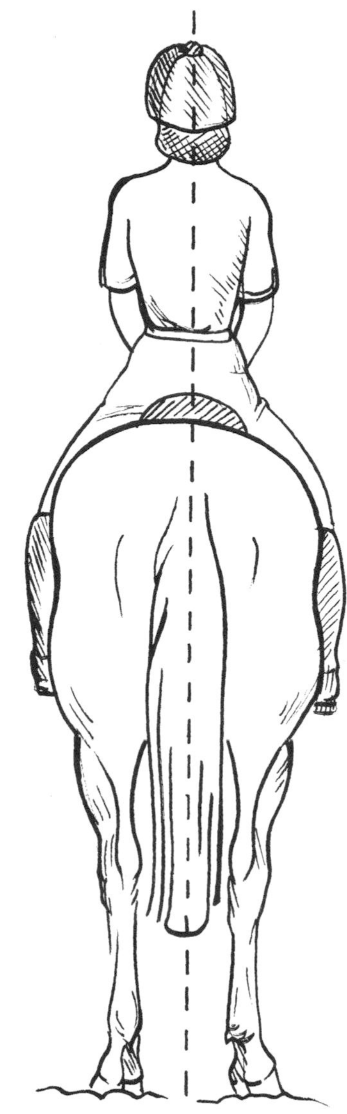

Fig. 6 Well balanced.

Fig. 7 Try carrying a small child on your shoulders.

of the heel and pass through the hip, elbow, shoulder and ear of the rider. If there is too much weight in front of the center line, as with a rider sitting on the fork (see fig. 8b), or with a rider who looks down, excess weight is placed over the horse's forehand. If there is too much weight behind the line, as with a rider possessing an armchair seat (see fig. 8c), the rider cannot sit deeply in the saddle. His legs tend to hang, rather ineffectively, down the sides of the horse.

Direct most of your weight onto your seat bones. To be more aware of the correct feeling place your hands underneath your seat bones and allow your weight to drop onto them. You should feel this weight pressing down on your hands. Take your hands away and still feel the weight of your body pushing onto the surface beneath, whether this be a saddle or chair. Keep your weight equally on these seat bones so as to stay in balance. Your legs should hang down as long as possible by the horse's sides.

A Fork Seat

Here the rider pushes the hips forwards and virtually sits on the fork of the legs (as in fig. 8b). He is not secure. With too much weight forward of the center line the horse can easily pull him out of the saddle by taking a hold or pulling on the reins. The seat has very little contact with the saddle. The angle of the body is wrong. It is impossible to relax into the rhythm of the horse. This seat is often caused by having the stirrups too long.

The Armchair Seat

This is the opposite of the fork seat because the rider puts too much weight on the area behind his seat bones close to the coccyx. The legs go forwards of the body, as if sitting in an armchair, and do not hang well down the horse's sides (see fig. 8c). Some of the rider's weight should pass down the legs, but with this seat it all stops at the saddle. The rider has to rely on the upper part of his body alone to achieve balance. The weight is behind the vertical, hence the rider is easily tipped backwards. This seat makes the rider insecure and he will often need to use the reins as a source of support. Stirrups that are too short may cause the rider to have an armchair seat.

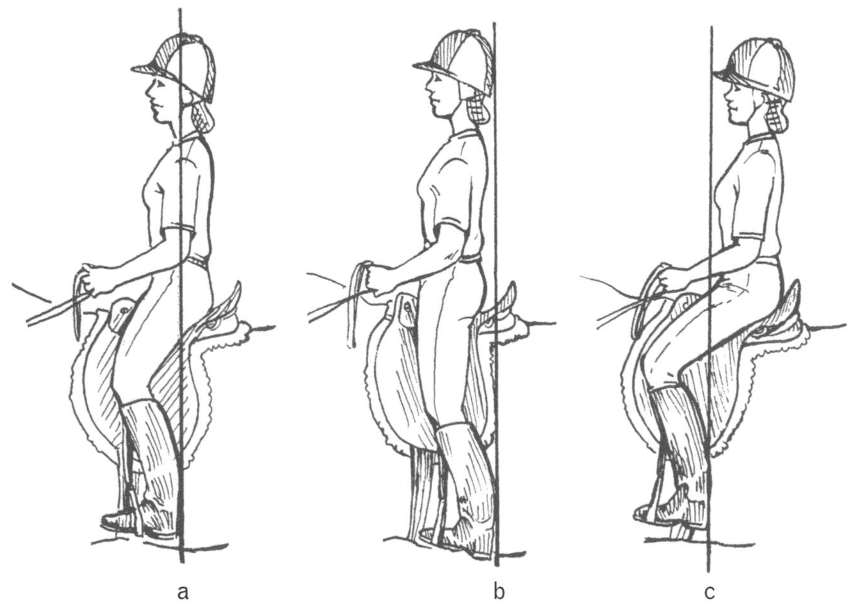

Fig. 8
a = Correct seat.
b = Fork seat.
c = Armchair seat.

GET SOMEONE TO LOOK AT YOU

Ask someone to look at you from the side and the back while you ride and check that you are sitting in a balanced position, as in figs. 6 and 8a. It is virtually impossible to tell if you are out of balance without such help, because you get so used to a position, even if it is wrong, and your body may have made unnoticed compensations ages ago.

WEIGHT OF THE HEAD

Many riders look down when they are riding, largely to check on what they and the horse are doing. Because we are so used to looking down we think nothing of it. In fact, the head weighs over 14 lbs and, if we are looking down, it seriously affects both our and the horse's balance. We are placing all this extra weight over the horse's forehand and therefore adding weight where we wish there to be less.

The Alexander Technique can be of enormous help in improving balance. It is a technique that is becoming much more popular and hence more available.

CHAPTER 12

The Balance of the Horse

As you may have noticed, the most evident difference between a horse and a human is that the human has two legs and the horse has four! This lies at the heart of the different factors governing the balance of the horse, compared with that of a person. Whereas the human, to be in balance, must have his weight evenly distributed over two legs, the horse spreads it over four. Ignore for now the lateral balance of the horse—that is the distribution of weight between the right and left sides. The most important matter is the lineal balance—the equal distribution of weight between the front legs, or the forehand, and the hind legs. The front legs carry a proportion of the weight, and the back legs the rest.

To be in balance, a horse should put the same weight on the front legs as on the back. But the horse normally puts far more weight on the front, yet doesn't feel out of balance. Because he has four legs, he isn't going to fall over, so he can quite happily keep his weight unevenly distributed. But this makes him very unathletic and cumbersome. One of the most important tasks a rider faces is to train the horse to carry the same weight on the back legs as on the front.

There are three reasons why most horses carry an excessive amount of weight on their forehand. Firstly, the shoulder, which is the heaviest single part of their anatomy, is almost immediately above the front legs. Secondly, the front legs also carry the head and neck, which are heavy as well. Thirdly, the weight of the rider is placed almost on top of those front legs (to sit any further back would put the horse's spine under strain). To correct this imbalance we must teach the horse to carry more of his weight with his hind legs. This is not easy for the horse nor is it easy for us to teach to him.

TRY IT YOURSELF

If you are interested to know how a horse feels with this extra weight on his forehand, you can get an idea of it by walking on all fours. Put your fists on the floor and walk with feet and hands as if a four-legged animal. I accept your front 'legs' are quite a lot shorter than the 'back' legs. By walking like this you are placing a vast amount of weight on your hands and very much more 'on the forehand' than any horse. In this position (fig. 9) you are very unathletic, as there is a terrific weight on your hands compared to that on your feet. Even though it is an exaggeration, it does give you some idea of how the horse feels. You couldn't imagine jumping a jump, or performing elegantly, with your body pinned down like this.

Remain on all fours. Instead of having your legs straight, gradually bend them and, at the same time, bring your feet under you. Have you noticed that the pres-

Fig. 9 On all fours.

sure, or weight, on your hands is reducing and at the same time your 'back' legs are taking more of the weight? Notice in fig. 10 how much your back has been lowered when you bring your legs further underneath you.

Your hands now feel lighter and freer: if you were a horse you would be better able to jump or look elegant. Now lower your back and bring your legs even further under your body; your hands should feel even lighter, as in fig. 11.

When you lower your back you put more of the weight of your body onto your legs. In the same way, the horse must learn to lower his quarters so that he moves more of his weight onto his back legs. When you put your legs under you and bend your knees (a human equivalent of hocks) this puts yet more weight on your legs, and less on your hands. In the same way the horse must learn to bend his hocks and put his back legs further under him. By combining all movements—lowering his back, bending his knees and putting his back legs further under him—he reduces further the weight his forehand is supporting, and increases that on his back legs.

Now that you have done this exercise and pretended to be a horse, can you imagine how much more athletic a horse must feel if he is able to lighten his forehand like this? You know how cumbersome you felt while walking on all fours. Hopefully it will give you a good indication of the difference we can make to our horse by training him to lower his quarters, bend his hocks and put them further under him. While you were in this position you will also have noticed that it puts strain on your calves and thighs. The horse finds this position hard, just as we do, and it takes a lot of training and exercise to make him strong enough to cope with it.

You have probably come across phrases such as "on the forehand", "lowering the quarters", "engaging the hindquarters", "engaging the hocks" and "balance of the horse" many times. Hopefully they make more sense to you now.

THE SHAPE OF THE HORSE'S SPINE

Most of our schooling is aimed towards this improvement of the balance of the horse. We use exercises that encourage the horse to step under himself. These exercises also round and stretch his back. How much work you will have to do to improve the balance of your horse will depend much on the raw material you are working with.

Fig. 10 Bring your feet under you.

Fig. 11 Bring your legs even further under your body.

Fig. 12 The balanced horse.

Fig. 13 The spine of a balanced horse.

THE BALANCED HORSE

There are some horses whose God-given conformation makes them naturally balanced. Their backs are already supple and rounded and their quarters naturally lower than their shoulders. When they move they are light and elegant. You can see that, as each front hoof hits the ground, it does so gently. It is obviously not carrying a great weight. The back legs come well under and each step is full of power. It creates a harmonious, beautiful picture. Notice how the body of the horse in fig. 12 is angled slightly upwards from the quarters to the shoulders. The spine of this horse from the poll (the top of the head between the ears) to the tail is rounded correctly. This allows the hind legs of the horse to come well under him and lift the front. The spine of this horse would look like fig. 13.

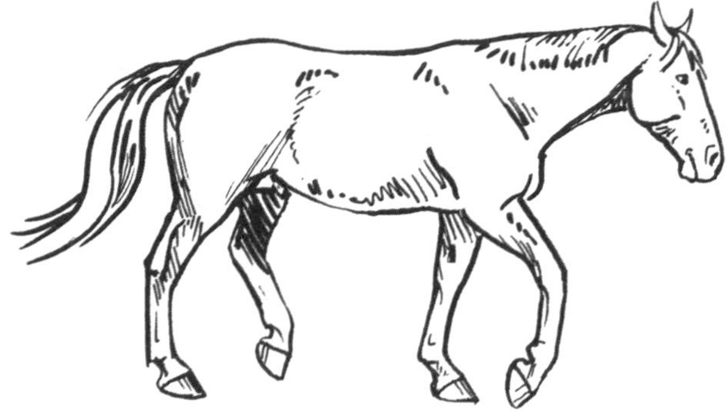

Fig. 14 The unbalanced horse.

THE UNBALANCED HORSE

Compare this now with a horse at the other end of the spectrum whose body is almost angled towards the forehand, as shown in fig. 14. The back is stiff and straight, the back legs barely coming under the horse, the nose poking forwards. You can see that much of the horse's weight is coming down on top of his front legs. If you look at the front legs of this horse you can see that as they hit the ground they are relatively heavy. Imagine how much of a strain these front legs are taking compared with the balanced horse. Visualize also how this horse must feel, unable to do anything vaguely athletic. It would be such an effort for him. The body of this horse slopes downwards from the back to the front. It is the opposite of the previous horse whose body is higher at the front.

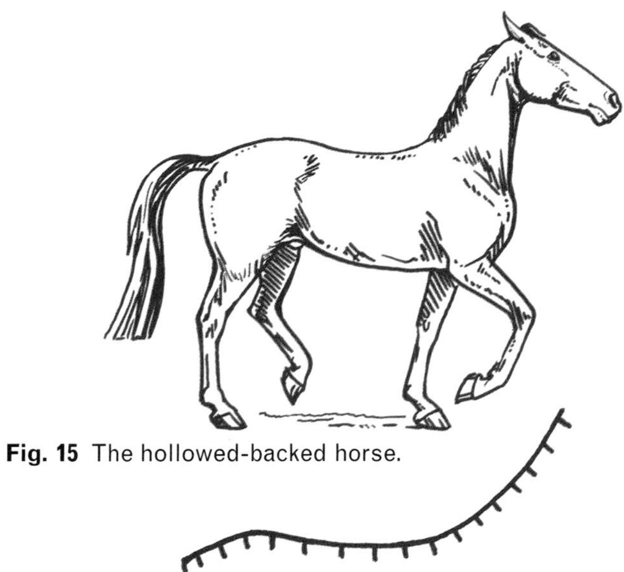

Fig. 15 The hollowed-backed horse.

Fig. 16 The spine of a hollowed-backed horse.

THE HOLLOWED-BACKED HORSE

There is another type of horse, while on the subject of balance, whose back is bent in entirely the wrong shape—that is, concave rather than convex. His head is probably thrown high into the air, his neck having to follow the hollow shape of his back. His gait may be short and staccato and his quarters and tail high. His back legs will barely come under his frame. See him in fig. 15. He will normally be heavy on his forehand but not always. Some horses, such as Arabs, hold their heads so high that they throw some of their weight backward onto the quarters. Their proud, arrogant stance and gait is beautiful and they move lightly over the ground. They are athletic, and many make fine jumpers, yet they are not going as well as they could. Unless they can be persuaded to alter the shape in which they hold their spine they can progress little. Some jumping ponies hold themselves in a similar shape, yet, by using themselves in this upside down manner, do achieve quite incredible results.

The back legs of these animals can never come under them. The concave spine means that their hind legs can only stick out behind them! These horses can never lower their quarters without changing the shape of their backs. Look how their quarters and tails are held high in the air. The concave shape of the spine (fig. 16) is the cause of this.

A major disadvantage of a horse whose spine is concave is that you cannot get him to accept the bit without altering the shape of his back. Because of the angle of the head and neck, the bit lies against the horse's lips, or between the molars and not on the bars of the mouth. This means that you will be less able to control him: there will be no stopping or harnessing power in the reins. Turns to the right or left will be easy enough, but you may well experience difficulty controlling the speed of a horse who goes like this. Because the bit doesn't lie against the bars of his mouth you cannot force him to stop. You are largely at the mercy of his good nature.

THE STRETCHY TOP LINE

Look at fig. 17. In drawing (a) the spine of the horse is concave. In drawing (b) the spine is convex, as it should be. If you were to measure the length of the spine in example (a) (the concave spine) and then measure the length of the spine in example (b) (the convex spine) you would find that spine (b) is considerably longer than (a), even though it is the same spine. Spine (a) is squashed together whereas the convex spine is stretched and measures more.

When you work a horse, envisage this imaginary line drawn from the nose to the poll, along the neck and back, and then down the back legs of the horse. I think of it as a stretchy

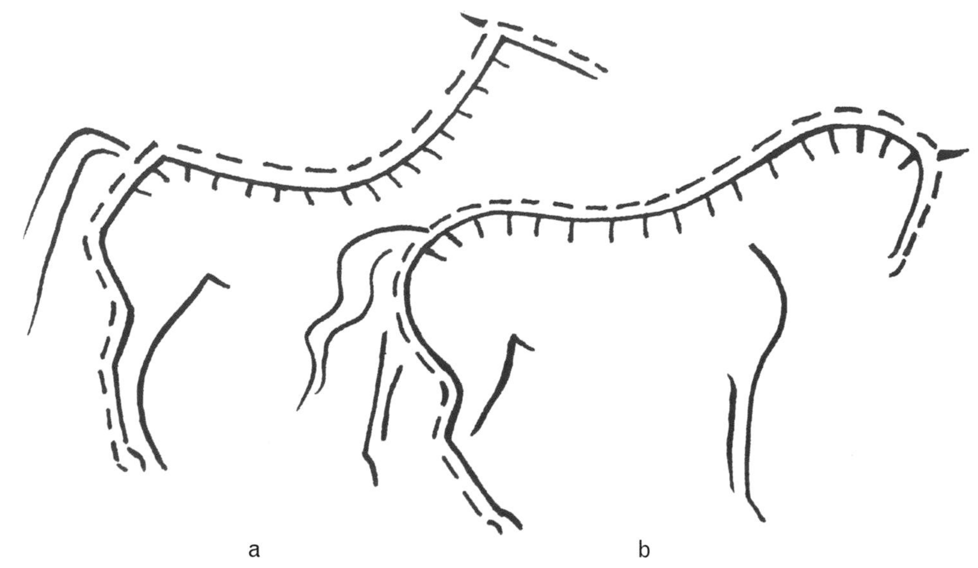

Fig. 17
a = Hollowed back.
b = Back rounded properly.

top line, though in truth it isn't really that stretchy, but stretch is what we want it to do. We need to make it become as long as possible. Using exercises which will make it stretch in different places, such as the neck, the back or the legs, makes the horse more supple along the whole length of this top line. When the spine has been stretched it allows the horse to step further under him and therefore carry more of his weight with his hind legs.

An apt comparison with the human frame would be the suppleness of our own spine. If you touch your toes with your fingers you can feel the back of your legs stretch and probably hurt, depending on your suppleness. If you touched your toes every day and pushed the limits of your ability to stretch, soon you would do it with ease. This is what we are going to persuade the horse to do. Not to touch his toes, to stretch his spine!

BEING ON THE BIT STRETCHES THE TOP LINE

We first help the horse to stretch his spine when we ask him to work on the bit. This particularly stretches the front part of the spine—the neck—but it does stretch the whole of the spine at the same time. After this, the exercises mostly involve movements that encourage the horse to step further under him so that he is stretching the back part of his spine and his back legs. Stretching any one part of the line more than it is usually stretched will affect all of the rest of the line, and make him feel that it too is being stretched. You may see the horse experience this when you ask for a transition, particularly into canter. The horse may be going nicely, but at the time of the transition he will want to lift his head in the air. This is because, if the transition is executed properly, it will have stretched part of the top line (that bit that wraps around his quarters and goes down his legs) as the horse steps under his weight. If he is insufficiently supple along his top line, he will lift his head in the air to release one part of the line, i.e. the front part, so that he is freer to stretch another part, i.e. the part that runs between his quarters and his hocks.

BEING MORE FORWARD GOING STRETCHES THE TOP LINE

If you ask the horse to be more forward going you will also be stretching the top line. This is because when the horse is more forward going he has to put his hocks further under him. If a horse is on the bit, but only just able to cope with the stretching this requires, he finds it much easier when the pace is slow. Working on the bit at walk is easy. If he is asked to be more forward going in walk he finds it more difficult to stay on the bit because the extra forward movement is making his hocks go further under him. You are stretching that top line at the back as well as the front. If you then ask for trot, as long as the trot is forward going, it will stretch the line even further. At canter it is even more so. This is particularly the case if your horse is jumping. He really has to put his hocks under him to lift his weight off the ground. Unless he is very supple along his top line, he needs a lot of freedom with his head and neck to take off.

We now return to the comparison between a balanced horse and an imbalanced one. Few horses are really well balanced—most are on their forehand to a greater or lesser degree. If you are choosing a horse, try to choose a balanced one. It will present much less work for you both in the future.

Fig. 18
Above: Catch your weight by putting your hands against the wall.
Below: The wall is too far away, so you have to put your foot forward.

The hollow-backed horse we described has even more work to do. Like most horses working incorrectly, he is very happy with the way he is going and is not disposed to change. Most of the work you do with him appears to make him less athletic. You are taking away the one advantage he had, his high head carriage, by asking him to lower his head and come onto the bit. It is demoralizing for you both because, for a long time, he will actually go worse and be less able to jump or move fluidly than he did before. Only when he has passed the stage where his back has rounded and stretched, and his legs are coming further under him, will either of you feel any benefit.

THE WALL

When a horse is imbalanced, the great weight on his forehand tends to push his nose down, towards the ground. Just as you felt heavy and cumbersome when you were on all fours, he is heavy and cumbersome in front. The weight driving him forwards makes it difficult for him to control his speed. As we know, the way for him to balance himself would be to put his back legs further under him. But, because he finds this difficult, he takes the easy option and remains imbalanced. To him it feels absolutely natural and the right way to go. If you try to control the speed by holding more tightly onto the reins, he will happily accept this and will lean on them. They are helping to support the weight of his forehand. Your hands are making life easier for him, but not for you! After a while your arms ache and the horse can never help himself to be better balanced while you are giving him this support.

To understand how the horse feels in this situation stand about three feet away from a wall. Allow yourself to tip forwards towards the wall. What do you instinctively do to stop yourself from falling over? You put your arms out and catch your weight by putting your hands on the wall.

Take a step backwards, so that you are about six feet away from the wall now. Again tip forwards towards the wall. You are falling over but the wall is too far away for you to reach it. What is your instinctive reaction this time? You put a foot forwards to catch your weight and to stop you from hitting the ground, as shown in fig. 18.

The wall acts very much as a strong rein contact would. It is there, so the horse will use it. Take it away and he has to put his legs under his weight to stop himself from falling forwards.

There are many exercises that will help him to stretch his frame, and put his back legs further under him, but the first thing you must do is remove the support of the reins. You must make him support himself and not allow him to have a strong contact. Your immediate reaction may be, "But, if I don't hold on to him with the reins, he will run away with me, or go faster than I want him to." Instead of maintaining a strong rein contact when he rushes, close your hands firmly on the reins, sit deep and squeeze your legs (all the aids for a downwards transition). As soon as he slows up release your strong contact. If he doesn't slow up use the above aids even more strongly. Never maintain a strong rein aid for longer than it takes for him to slow up. As soon as the horse begins to go at the pace you require, lighten the contact. If he speeds up again, which he probably will, repeat the process. You will probably have to do it many, many times before he not only understands what you mean but is prepared to put the effort into carrying his own weight.

It is easier to try the above in a confined area such as an arena. The horse will know that the perimeter fencing means he will have to regulate his speed unless he wishes to crash into it—which he won't. It also means that you, the rider, can relax in the more secure surroundings.

Photo Credits and Captions

PAGE ii-iii ©RO-MA Stock /Index Stock

PAGE iv ©Omni Photo Communications, Inc / Index Stock

PAGE vi-vii ©B Gillingham /Index Stock

PAGE viii-ix ©Michele Burgess /Index Stock

PAGE x ©Geoff Hansen /Valley News, "Ribbons are lined up for winners among the 82 horses in the events at the Morgan Heritage Days at the Tunbridge, Vermont Fairgrounds. The event has been held annually since 1982."

PAGE 1 ©Geoff Hansen, "Thirteen-year-old Rochelle Vanderwende brushes Roty in preparation for a lesson at Hitching Post Farm in South Royalton, Vermont."

PAGE 3 ©Bob Jacobson /Index Stock

PAGE 4 ©Geoff Hansen, "Seven-year-old Abe Adams leads his pony Toby across the field in Strafford, Vermont. Anne Adams said she bought a pony for her son because riding gives kids 'a feeling of power and accomplishment, and more important, gives them a chance to develop a friendship with an animal.'"

PAGE 5 ©Geoff Hansen, "Fifteen-year-old Heather Spain grooms her Morgan horse, Razz in South Royalton, Vermont. Spain has been riding for ten years, and does all of the work required to keep a horse."

PAGE 6-7 ©David Frazier /Index Stock

PAGE 8 ©Ernest Manewal /Index Stock

PAGE 10 ©Geoff Hansen, "Nellie, left, and Dixie enjoy a brisk winter morning while romping around in the snow."

PAGE 11 ©Geoff Hansen, "Navajo horses exercise between the cliffs of Canyon de Chelly near Chinle, Arizona. The canyon, located on the Navajo Indian Reservation, is 26 miles long and still has the stone cliff dwellings of Pueblo people from 2,000 years ago. The Navajo today use the canyon's flatlands to cultivate crops."

PAGE 12 ©Cantock Images, Inc. /Index Stock

PAGE 13 ©RO-MA Stock /Index Stock

PAGE 14-15 ©Bob Trehearne /Index Stock

PAGE 16 ©B Gillingham /Index Stock

PAGE 17 ©Zefa Visual Media, Germany's Collection /Index Stock

PAGE 19 ©Geoff Hansen, "Earl Silloway of Strafford leads his Belgian draft horse Peaches out of the barn to hitch her up to the sleigh for a ride. Silloway, who has had horses off and on over the years, started a business with his draft horses in 1990."

PAGE 20-21 ©Diapho Agency's Collection /Index Stock

PAGE 23 ©David Trask /Index Stock

PAGE 24 ©RO-MA Stock /Index Stock

PAGE 25 ©Diaphor Agency /Index Stock

PAGE 27 ©Geoff Hansen, "Heather Spain talks to Razz while grooming him. Spain rides the six-year-old horse in dressage competition."

PAGE 28-29 ©Geoff Hansen, "Rollie Olson of Plainfield, New Hampshire, readies gelding, Flash, for training in western riding at Lasting View Morgans. Olson and her family started the farm, where they board horses and give lessons, in 1998."

PAGE 30 ©Henry Horenstein /Index Stock

PAGE 31 ©Allen Russell /Index Stock

PAGE 32 ©Geoff Hansen, "Before starting her training with Flash, Rollie Olson exercises him on a lead."

PAGE 33 ©Geoff Hansen, "Rollie Olson trains Flash, a national champion in western riding as a three- and four-year-old."

PAGE 34-35 ©Eddie Stangler /Index Stock

PAGE 36 ©Geoff Hansen, "Elroy, a Percheron gelding, eats hay at Earl Silloway's farm."

PAGE 37 ©Jeffrey Blackman /Index Stock

PAGE 38 ©Geoff Hansen, "Driver Alex Greer of Springfield, Vermont, waits with his team of Percheron draft horses, Kincaid, right, and Steve, for the bride and her party to board a carriage going to a wedding in South Woodstock, Vermont. Greer is known at fairs in Northern New England for the eight-horse hitch he does in the show ring. In addition to going to weddings and parades with the horses, Greer and his wife Barb also give sleigh and hay rides on their farm."

PAGE 39 ©Geoff Hansen, "Dixie, a quarter-horse, eats hay taken from property next to pasture where the horses graze."

PAGE 40 ©Geoff Hansen, "While Leslie Bancroft Haynes unhitches the harness, Hannah Polson gives Welsh pony, Ally Oop, a pat after his carriage training at Haynes' Rough Terrain Farm in Randolph Center, Vermont. Ally Oop is being trained for competitive carriage and pleasure driving."

PAGE 42 ©Geoff Hansen/Valley News, "Carl Vance, 15, leads his Belgian work horse, Beauty, across a pasture in South Royalton, as they help telephone company workers install copper cable. Beauty has helped the company drag line through woods, over rivers and even through snow up to her belly. Vance had lived with an Amish family in Ohio earlier in the summer to learn more about working with draft horses.

PAGE 43 ©Geoff Hansen, "Leslie Bancroft Haynes gives Hannah Polson direction on holding Boomer while harnessing him for carriage. Polson moved back to Vermont to work on Haynes' farm after spending a year on a Kentucky horse farm."

PAGE 44 ©Canstock Images, Inc /Index Stock

PAGE 45 ©Allen Russell /Index Stock

PAGE 46-47 ©RO-MA Stock /Index Stock

PAGE 49 ©Tim Haske /Index Stock

PAGE 50 ©Geoff Hansen/Valley News, "Belgian draft horse team Scotty and Teddy rub noses at the Billings Farm and Museum in Woodstock, Vermont. Work horses were an integral part of the farm's dairy and forestry operation a century ago, and are still used on the farm today."

PAGE 51 ©Geoff Hansen/Valley News, "Originally used for milking dairy cows, a historic round barn in North Tunbridge, Vermont, is now home to horses."

PAGE 53 ©Chip Henderson /Index Stock

PAGE 54 ©Geoff Hansen, "With bridesmaid Katie Bunn-Marcuse standing at her side, bride Blakeley A. Murrell-Liland leans over to kiss her Arabian horse, BJ, before her wedding near the family farm in South Woodstock. Murrell-Liland got the horse from her parents as a present while she was in high school, when she did competitive trail riding."

PAGE 55 ©Geoff Hansen, "Arabian mare Molly Rocket grazes among the chickens. Owner Sylvia Spain learned to ride as a child growing up on Long Island. In later years, Spain worked as an exercise rider at racetracks in California, Florida, New York and West Virginia."

PAGE 56 ©Geoff Hansen, "Earl Silloway's Belgian draft horses, Peaches, right, and Cream, are set to go for a ride."

PAGE 57 ©Henry Horenstein /Index Stock

PAGE 58 ©Geoff Hansen, "A young rider takes her horse out for some exercise on a cold late fall day."

PAGE 59 ©Geoff Hansen, "Fourteen-year-old Rose Komorowski rides Thunder in a lesson at the Hitching Post Farm in South Royalton. Komorowski has been riding for the past six years."

PAGE 60 ©Geoff Hansen, "Ten-year-old Allegra Walters leads her Wesh cob pony Crossroads Traveler out of the riding ring following a training session at Rough Terrain Farm in Randolph Center, Vermont. Walters has owned the horse for about six months."

PAGE 61 ©Geoff Hansen, "Veterinarian Heather Hoyns examines Rubin, a Hanoverian, while visiting Appledore Farm in Hartland, Vermont. Owner Daphne Preece was preparing to take two of her horses to Florida over the winter. Hoyns works out of her van, visiting farms within a 25-mile radius of Kedron Valley Veterinary Clinic in South Woodstock, Vermont, where she is based."

PAGE 62 ©Geoff Hansen/Valley News, "An owner holds onto his miniature horse before the start of the Woodstock Wassail Celebration. The Christmas celebration's parade with horses is an annual tradition in the Vermont town."

PAGE 64 ©Carl Purcell /Index Stock

PAGE 65 ©Frank Siteman /Index Stock

PAGE 66 ©Geoff Hansen, "Seventeen-year-old Kylie Lyman pets her thoroughbred Puck, a horse she has owned for three years."

PAGE 67 ©Geoff Hansen, "Hannah Polson holds Boomer in place while he is harnessed for carriage training at Rough Terrain Farm in Randolph Center, Vermont. Polson works and lives on the farm where she did her mentorship as a senior in high school."

PAGE 68-69 ©Stewart Cohen /Index Stock

PAGE 70 ©Allen Russell /Index Stock

PAGE 71 ©RO-MA Stock /Index Stock

PAGE 73 ©Ellen Skye /Index Stock

PAGE 74 ©Ernest Manewal /Index Stock

PAGE 75 ©Phil Lauro /Index Stock

PAGE 77 ©Geoff Hansen, "With his friend May Conley, 10, watching, Lucas Thomashow, 10, feeds Storm, foreground, and Dixie, in Strafford. Thomashow has been riding horses with his family since moving to Vermont from Brooklyn three years ago."

PAGE 78 ©Geoff Hansen, "Hannah Polson works with Ally Oop. The pony is being trained for competitive carriage and pleasure driving. Polson works and lives on the farm."

PAGE 79 ©Geoff Hansen, "Rollie Olson enters the indoor riding arena with Flash."

PAGE 81 ©Jeff Greenberg /Index Stock

PAGE 82 ©Bud Freund /Index Stock

PAGE 83 ©Wilson Goodrich /Index Stock

PAGE 84 ©Allen Russell /Index Stock

PAGE 85 ©Frank Siteman /Index Stock

PAGE 86-87 ©Charles Shoffner /Index Stock

PAGE 88 ©Geoff Hansen

PAGE 90 ©Geoff Hansen, "Thirteen-year-old Kaley Maxfield readies her quarterhorse Alex for a lesson and ride at the Hitching Post Farm. She has been riding horses for eight years."

PAGE 91 ©Geoff Hansen, "Drawings by riding students hang on the walls of the office of Lasting View Morgans. The Olson family built the farm in 1998."

PAGE 92 ©Peter Walton /Index Stock

PAGE 93 ©Geoff Hansen/Valley News, "A couple takes a break to enjoy the fall foliage during the Box B Ranch Trail Ride in East Corinth, Vermont. The annual event draws riders from across New England."

PAGE 94-95 ©Inga Spence /Index Stock

PAGE 96 ©Charlie Berland /Index Stock

PAGE 97 ©HIRB /Index Stock

PAGE 98-99 ©Geoff Hansen

PAGE 100 ©Geoff Hansen, "As Carl Russell chains his load of sugar maples to the bobsled in Bethel, Vermont, draft horses Benjamin, right, and Peg wait patiently to go to work. Benjamin is an eight-year-old European Belgian and Peg is a North American Belgian in her mid-twenties."

PAGE 101 ©Geoff Hansen, "Leslie Bancroft Haynes works with Boomer as he pulls a wooden drag, part of carriage training at Haynes' Rough Terrain Farm. Haynes, who started the farm from the ground up in 1990, has a hand in virtually all aspects of the horse culture, including plans to build a bed and breakfast that will cater to handicapped riders."

PAGE 103 ©Geoff Hansen, "Cream, a Belgian draft horse, shows off Earl Silloway's finest harness before going out for a ride."

PAGE 104 ©Grantpix /Index Stock

PAGE 106 ©Geoff Hansen, "With her dog Samantha at her side, Rollie Olson mounts Flash."

PAGE 107 ©Geoff Hansen/Valley News, "John Hammond turns another row of soil with his family of Suffolk horses during the Moonstruck Farm Plowing Match in Piermont, New Hampshire. While at the match, Hammond's mare bred with her mate and later gave birth to "Plowman's Nick." Hammond also won the match."

PAGE 108-109 ©Omni Photo /Index Stock

PAGE 110 ©Allen Russell /Index Stock

PAGE 111 ©Tim O'Hara /Index Stock

PAGE 112 ©Geoff Hansen, "Owen, a Dutch Warmblood, grazes on Anne Adams' property."

PAGE 113 ©Tim O'Hara /Index Stock

PAGE 114-115 ©Mark Barrett /Index Stock

PAGE 116 ©Paul Gallaher /Index Stock

PAGE 118 ©Geoff Hansen, "Carl Russell harnesses his Belgian draft horses (not pictured) before taking them out logging. Russell has been logging with horses since 1986."

PAGE 119 ©B Gillingham /Index Stock

PAGE 120 ©Peggy Koyle /Index Stock

PAGE 121 ©Phil Lauro /Index Stock

PAGE 122 ©RO-MA Stock /Index Stock

PAGE 124 ©Peter Walton /Index Stock

PAGE 125: ©Mark Barrett /Index Stock

PAGE 126 ©RO-MA Stock /Index Stock

PAGE 127 ©Frank Conaway /Index Stock

PAGE 128 ©Sandy Clark /Index Stock

PAGE 129 ©RO-MA Stock /Index Stock

PAGE 131 ©Mark Barrett /Index Stock

PAGE 132 ©Henry Horenstein /Index Stock

PAGE 133 ©Geoff Hansen, "Abe Adams and his pony. Anne Adams said she taught her son to ride because 'I figure that knowing how to ride a horse is like knowing how to ice skate or drive stick shift: You never know when it might come in handy.'"

PAGE 134 ©IT Stock Int'l /Index Stock

PAGE 135 ©Geoff Hansen, "Teenagers, from left, Kaley Maxfield, Kate Ripley, and Kylie Lyman ride their horses back to Hitching Post Farm. The trio had just finished a lesson on the farm and took their horses down the road to cool them down."

PAGE 136 ©Chad Ehlers /Index Stock

PAGE 154-155 ©Chris Minerva /Index Stock

PAGE 164-165 ©Zefa Visual Media /Index Stock

PAGE 166 ©Geoff Hansen/Valley News, "A draft horse finds shelter in the shade of a doorway in the barnyard of a West Claremont, New Hampshire, farm."

INDEX

T

V

W